The Tiger Tamer

TODD L. SHULER

The Tiger Tamer by Todd Shuler
Published by Tora Publishing
(a division of Crown Global Corporation)
223 Wimbledon Place
Macon, GA 31211

ISBN: 0-9889589-1-0
ISBN-13: 978-0-9889589-1-3

For Worldwide Distribution
Printed in the U.S.A.

For more information, call (404) 939-0807
Or e-mail: t3book@gmail.com

DEDICATION

To my great managers and mentors
who cared enough to lead by example and were willing to patiently guide
my career through their practical and insightful advice.

To those of you entering the workforce for the first time or transitioning
into new careers, I hope you find "The Tiger Tamer" to be one of the most
entertaining and insightful career self-management books you'll ever read.
Then, pass it along to someone else. (smile)

Table of Contents

ACKNOWLEDGMENTS

My many friends and colleagues (past and present) who
read my short story "A View from the Cage"
and encouraged me to write
The Tiger Tamer.

INTRODUCTION - THE TALE OF THE TIGER

The Tamer and the Ferocious Cat is a circus act that never ceases to delight audiences who wait in almost feverish anticipation. Danger fills the air as the tamer enters the cage. He glides around the cage with ease, cracking his whip and bending the tiger to his will. Snarling, the tiger reveals razor-sharp teeth as he watches the tamer circling him with rapt attention. When the tamer closes in, the tiger immediately swipes his heavy paw at the man, eyes blazing in outrage at the tamer's audacity in approaching him. The audience gasps, watches in stunned silence and then breaks out into heavy applause as the ferocious animal gives in and obeys his master's commands. To the audience, the tamer is undoubtedly in control; the tamer, however, knows different.

The tamer understands that the tiger is much bigger and stronger than he is. He also knows that even if he nurtured a tiger from birth to maturity, the animal will never truly be tamed. The same animal, whose head he's patted, back he's stroked, and mouth he's fed countless times, can turn on him in a moment's notice. In an instant, the tiger may pounce upon the tamer. The trainer respects the tiger's nature and never forgets that the tiger, sleeping or awake, always poses a direct threat.

This is the inherent danger in working with a tiger and a tamer never really works alone. Entranced by watching the Tiger Tamer at work, the audience may never see the silent crew that works inconspicuously outside of the cage

1

to ensure everyone's safety and a successful performance. The tamer keeps his eyes locked upon the tiger. His crew is always beside him, moving props in and out, opening and closing doors, and keeping treats accessible for the tamer to give the tiger. The tamer's crew at times may also distract the tiger so the tamer can rest a moment and catch his breath. In an emergency, the crew can step in and assist the tamer instantly, saving his life and preventing injury. Just like the tamer keeps his eyes focused upon the tiger, the crew also is constantly aware of the nature of the tiger.

You may not have considered it, but your business a lot like that tiger. Think about it. Whether your business is a startup or has been charging along for months or years, your project has the same appetite and unpredictability. Respect it. Never take your eyes off of it. You need your crew's support; you must treat them well and should never step in the cage without them on the other side.

Just like the Tiger Tamer who recognizes the challenge in training and working with a tiger everyday, you too can learn how to manage and run your own business. Running a business is a lot like being a Tiger Tamer because your business can be unpredictable and take you into uncharted waters. Just like the Tiger Tamer at the circus needs a support crew he can count on, you too will need a team of professional, skilled individuals who you treat well and who respect you and work well together.

This book is intended for new and seasoned working professionals, entrepreneurs or restarting a career after many years away from the marketplace. It will help you fulfill your role as the Tiger Tamer, both inside the cage and out. You'll learn how to make your presence known, crack the whip when appropriate and act decisively without fear. Through hard work and consistent effort over time, you will discover that you and your team can tame your tiger, achieve the results you're striving for and may even teach your tiger a few tricks. When you've mastered how to tame your tiger, you'll be able to attract an excited audience that buys tickets and fill the circus tent or in business terms, build a loyal consumer fan base that is eager to see your next product release.

1 - THE GREATEST SHOW ON EARTH

The show was over, and people were spilling out of the tent into the dusk. Martino "Tino" Velazquez left his seat in the bleachers, following a host of tired parents and over-stimulated kids, stepping over the rainbow-colored mess of dropped ice cream cones and smashed cotton candy on the floor. His head was spinning. Tino hadn't been to the circus in years. He bought a ticket for tonight's show on a whim, showed up expecting to laugh at the cheesiness of it all, and ended up finding it every bit as amazing as his memory of the first one his parents had taken him to at the age of 5. He laughed wholeheartedly like the kindergarteners at the clowns. He held his breath watching the acrobats on the trapeze and the juggler and his buzzing chainsaws. When the big cats loped into the center ring, driven by a laughing, mysterious man called "Rajah" in red leather and black silk, Tino's jaw fell open, just like it had when he was five. He watched the Tamer moving fearlessly between his tigers, patting their glossy sides, directing them through flaming hoops, smiling confidently. The animals were huge and muscular; their eyes glittered fiercely, but they did exactly what he said. Tino thought to himself, **That is what I want to do with my life**.

He lay awake that night thinking about it, sure it was a completely crazy idea, but unable to dismiss it. Just before falling asleep, he remembered reading something Apple's legendary founder Steve Jobs once said:

Remembering that you are going to die is the best way I know to avoid the trap of thinking you have something to lose. You are already naked. There is no reason not to follow your heart.[i]

At 8 a.m. the next morning, Tino arrived at the travel camper that served as the main office. He stood across the desk from the Ringmaster, a tall and broad-shouldered woman who was now looking at him with mild amusement in her eyes. This was Leila Martin, also known as, "Lovely Leila Maravilla." She owned Cirque Maravilla. It had belonged to her parents before her, and she was now the proud matriarch of the family business. She held Tino's resume in her hands and spent a moment looking it over. She looked up at him, and said, "You know how many people knock on my office door each year wanting to run away and join the circus?" Tino shrugged. "Dozens. You know how many stay for more than a few weeks when I do give them a shot? Almost none. You've got a college degree, kid! Majored in business, which ought to make your parents happy. Why on earth do you want to work here?"

Tino was ready for the question. "You're right. I did what they wanted me to do when I picked that degree. But I never wanted to wear a suit or sell widgets. I want to do something to challenge myself. Something really unique." She was already shaking her head slightly, so he picked up speed and gestured broadly. "Look at my resume - I'm a responsible guy. I was an officer in two important campus organizations. I'm smart. My grades were good. I'm creative - I even did stand-up comedy for beer money on the weekends. I can handle surprises and even pretty gross stuff; I was a volunteer adventure leader for high school kids. Have you ever had to unstop a plugged camp latrine? I just want to do something for myself before I have to sell my soul to a corporation."

Leila laughed loud. "Kid, don't you know that a circus is a business, too? Think I live on the smiles of little children? Or feed the animals on joy and sunshine? I've got the same worries and responsibilities as any other entrepreneur or manager. I just do it in sequined tights." I laughed. "My relationship with this circus is not that different from Rajah's work with those tigers of his." She stared at Tino.

Tino gave it one more try. He said, "I'll work anywhere you want me to. I'll sweep, I'll sell popcorn, I'll scoop elephant poop and feed the camel antacids. I really want to work here."

Leila stuck her right hand in her pant pocket and rotated her head slowly, looking a lot like Tino's dad did when his employees were annoying. She sighed, "Ok, Martino Velazquez. I've got an opening for general crew since Pete married that piano teacher and stayed behind in Virginia. You *have a week to pack up, sell your car, and sublet your apartment. Meet us in Buffalo, NY next Friday. I'll e-mail you with more instructions; you'll have to pay your own way there. See you then."*

Tino was clearly being dismissed, and he wanted to get out of there quick before he said something dumb that made her change her mind. He nodded with as much dignity as he could muster, grabbed the doorknob, and walked out with a simple, "Thanks. I'll see you next Friday." As soon as he was sure he was out of earshot, he shouted and took off running towards his car. **I'm joining the circus!** *he thought, almost dizzy with excitement.* **Ha ha! Can you believe it? Wait 'till those tigers get a load of me!** *He could hear the roaring of the crowds already.*

✍ ✍ ✍ ✍

Being in charge of a business, whether you are the owner, CEO, CFO or Vice President, sounds great on paper and even better over coffee or a drink. But, if you're an entrepreneur, manage a good-sized business, or have administrative responsibility in another organization, you might experience a lot of moments where you feel like Leila Martin. While the public may be seduced by the bright lights or the slick packaging that your brand displays, they do not realize how you're backstage carrying the weight of the world on your shoulders. On chaotic days, when you face thousands of decisions to make and have to satisfy the needs of multiple individuals, you might really feel like your work *is* a circus. You're just about to be eaten by one of those tigers.

It's easy to go from excited to overwhelmed. But being overwhelmed does not mean that you have to give up your plan or relinquish control of your business. You don't have to feel like you fell out of the driving seat and are hanging on for dear life as your business rushes forward to meet demands like one of those cars rushing dangerously headlong down the racetrack. Running a business does not have to be a life or death situation every day or feel precarious and stressful constantly. The purpose of this book is to help professionals like you move from feeling that clowns are running the show to becoming a tiger tamer in the Greatest Show on Earth. In the Tale of the Tiger, I explain how businesses are like big cats – they're powerful, unpredictable, and ultimately, untamable. No one can truly handle a tiger alone. You also should not take your eyes off of one for even a minute. However, with preparation, focus, and expert assistance, you can bend the tiger to your will and give people a heart-stopping experience.

Tino Velazquez, our young hero, only dreams of becoming the star of the show. But if he wants to be the star, he's going to have to learn a few major lessons and get to know the circus inside and out. Fortunately, the Cirque Maravilla has a few seasoned mentors who are willing to show him the ropes. If you are willing to join them on the journey, they might have a little wisdom for you too. Through this simple allegory, we will address key questions for the leadership of organizations such as:

- How do you develop and communicate a vision?
- What does it take to build effective teams?
- How do you get everyone on the same page about a SWOT?
- How do you execute on plans and quickly assess whether these plans are working effectively?

You may be a middle manager on the cusp of moving up, or an administrator tasked with expanding your company's base of influence. Maybe you are employed at a business generating $350 to $800 million in annual sales or the owner of a business this size. Perhaps you're an entrepreneur with a small start up, a large non-profit or like Leila Martin, you've inherited a family business. Maybe you are a student who hopes someday to join one of these organizations. It doesn't really matter — everyone has tigers to tame and dreams of occupying the center ring. This story and this book are here to assist you in getting there. So without further ado…

Ladies and gentlemen, leaders of all ages, welcome to our show!

2 - YOUR TIGER, YOUR BUSINESS

Tino stretched his arms and arched his back, was rewarded by a chorus of popping noises. Boy, was he stiff. My body sounds like that machine, *he thought, swinging open the door of the popcorn truck and stepping out into the night. The crowds had long gone home, and he wanted some air before he started in on the clean-up process. He'd been on concessions duty for three weeks, and it was a terrible bore. He now hated the smell of cotton candy and never wanted to eat another ice cream sandwich. But he knew better than to complain. This was a disciplinary assignment, and he was very aware that he had earned this penance.*

His first six weeks with the circus had gone well. He showed up in Buffalo early and was waiting at the site when the circus trucks pulled in. If Leila was surprised to see him, she didn't show it. She just assigned him a bunk with five other guys in one of the campers, lassoed a clown (sans make up) to show him around, and said, "Have Naeglin find him something to do." They put him on KP, and for the first week he had served eggs and enchiladas in the staff canteen tent. He had played it just right—been friendly to everyone, quick to finish tasks, just happy to be part of the show. Next Monday Leila had walked in, said "Put down the potato peeler and come with me," and introduced him to Franz, the prop master. He learned how to stack boxes, assemble risers, organize hoops and batons by size and color, clean the dog drool off of red rubber balls, and why you never, _never_ touch Rita the bareback rider's flags. The week after that, he had been with the foreman, Ed Naeglin, helping assemble the tents and rigging. Then there was a week with Connor and the juggling crew, figuring out that tuning chainsaws was not one of his strengths.

By then he thought he'd figured out what was going on. Most of the other staff members were in stable jobs—performers, crew members, support staff, drivers, food handlers. A few of them did double duty, but they didn't bounce around so much. Leila must be watching him, sussing out his strengths and limitations. He thought he could live with that, and would wait for the right moment to introduce himself to the tiger tamer and his crew. So he was delighted when they sent him over to Sergei, the "animal boss" and staff veterinarian. And that had gone well, too. He learned how to properly feed and water the camels and elephants. He helped Eileen and Sam flea dip their whole *pack of wiggling, yapping dogs. He scooped a lot of poop. A LOT of poop. And learned how to properly dispose of it to so local authorities in each town had no reason to complain. He was really enjoying it. The animal people were nice overall; it was clear they loved and respected their beasts. Eileen and Sam really understood dog behavior, and he was impressed that they kept all of those canines motivated and focused without any rough treatment or yelling. He liked that Rita and her crew kept their horses clean, tended their hoofs and mouths with care, and kept them calm and docile backstage. Sergei and Annabeth performed with the elephants; as Tino followed her around with a bucket each day, Annabeth would tell him all about elephant behavior in the wild, and her work with an animal sanctuary in Florida.*

The tigers were still a mystery, though. They were kept away from the other beasts, as even their smell made the horses edgy. Their crew was tight-knit. They built the enclosures themselves, fed and cleaned up with no outside help. They spent hours together, working and talking, laughing at private jokes. Only Sergei was allowed to approach, when the tigers got their weekly check-up. Raj, the tamer, was tall and olive-skinned; every afternoon he spent in the enclosure, wrestling with the beasts one at a time, petting them, tossing them scraps. He looked so at ease with them, and they bounded around him like Eileen and Sam's dogs. Tino could have watched that for hours, so captivated he couldn't have told anyone how many crew members were hanging around outside the enclosure, who was there, or what they were doing. And that was his mistake.

Looking back, Tino knew that he'd been very stupid, that he should have paid closer attention to what was going on. Sergei had called for Tino to grab a box and follow him to the tigers' enclosure; it was vaccination time. Finally! *He thought, scrambling to follow. When they had arrived, Sergei had instructed him to stay put and followed Raj in. The tiger crew ignored him, keeping their eyes on the action in the cage, loosely gripping long poles. Sergei and Raj moved from cat to cat, inspecting eyes and mouths, Raj keeping their attention while Sergei swiftly poked a hypodermic into a flank. Tino watched one of the cats rub its side against the bars, scratching an itch. Its tail snaked out of the cage, and he thought* Here's my chance to pet a tiger. *He stole a little closer, reached out his hand…and the tiger turned. It twitched its nostrils. It narrowed its eyes. It raised its tail higher….and a spray of urine hit Tino straight in the eyes!*

Tino had stumbled back, coughing and sputtering, his nostrils on fire. He tripped over the box and fell down. That got everyone's attention—Sergei, Raj, and the tigers included—and everything else happened fast. Someone yanked him to his feet, and dragged him away from the enclosure. The crew quickly turned their attention back to the cage, but the tigers seemed unconcerned. Sergei and Raj stepped out, securing the door behind them. The guy holding his arm, Dan, was the assistant tamer. Dan started to yell, "What were you doing that close to the enclosure, stupid? Ever heard about not making any sudden moves or noises around wild animals?" He was clearly gearing up for a vigorous ass-chewing, but Raj called his name. As they approached, Sergei asked, "Tino, did you muck out the camels' straw this morning like I asked?" Rubbing his burning eyes, Tino replied, "Yeah, of course." The two men started to laugh, and Raj said, "You may want to wash the camel pee off your pants before you get near the big cats next time, Tino. Calm down, Dan. Nobody got hurt." Raj clapped Dan on the shoulder and they started away, Dan giving Tino one more baleful look before he left.

No one had seen Tino reach for the tiger, and Sergei had told him not to worry, but that afternoon he got the message to report to concessions, and he had been there ever since. No one had mentioned the incident specifically, though the jokes about his "Tiger cologne" had been plentiful for the next few days. Between handing out hot dogs and making change, there had been a lot of time to reflect on that moment and on what could have happened instead. He was thinking about it now, when a figure stepped out of the dark. It was Raj. "Any popcorn left?" he asked, casually.

He took the paper bag that Tino offered, sat on the trailer steps, and gestured for Tino to join him. "Tigers are really beautiful animals, aren't they?" Raj said, quietly. Tino nodded. "The crowds love them. And they love me because they see those claws and teeth, and think I've got those cats under my thumb. I pat their heads, point at the hoops, and they jump. It's my job to make people think that. But for the crew and me, the reality is different. I've raised those three cats from the time they were cubs. They know me, they trust me, and I love each one. But I also know that any one of them is capable of killing or maiming me in a second. Because they aren't like Eileen and Sam's dogs. They are single-minded predators, and those instincts can take over at any time, if some small thing changes and the tiger gets spooked."

Tino looked up, eyes wide. He had never thought about that before. Raj went on, "What my crew does is a lot more complicated than anyone thinks. The crowd just sees me and the tigers. They just think about how much fun we are to watch. They don't think about the fact that we have 10 minutes to assemble a cage to keep them all safe. They're busy watching the trapeze. They don't notice Dan and the others running around the edge of the ring, moving props, watching me, distracting the cats when I need a breather. But we plan it carefully, and I know where my guys are at every moment. Because if one of the cats turns on me, I'm counting on them to pull me out and keep me from bleeding to death. Every move those guys make is to keep me safe, keep the audience safe, and keep the cats safe. Every day. In the ring and out. When Dan yelled at you, he was worried that all the noise you made could have put me or Sergei in harm's way."

Tino buried his face in his hands, "Man, I'm so sorry…" But Raj smiled. "Leila doesn't let just anybody run away and join our circus. If you're with us, you must have something going for you. But the choices you make on the road are what really counts. Sergei says you're good with the other animals. Get any free time on concessions detail? Why don't you read this and come see me when you're done?" He pulled a paperback book from his back pocket, tossed it on the steps and stood. "Thanks for the popcorn." And then Raj was gone. Tino picked up the book. <u>Tiger Anatomy and Behavior</u>. For the first time in weeks, he felt his spirits start to rise.

✔ ✔ ✔ ✔

Tino's a-ha moment is the same one that all would-be leaders have to have: to every organization there is a front stage and a backstage; once you go behind that curtain, your whole perspective has to change. Your audience— customers, clients, patrons, whatever form they take—is looking for a seamless experience. In order to give it to them, you have to work incredibly hard, with planning and intentionality, in order to make it look easy. Leaders have to think about and maintain two distinct visions for success, one onstage for the audience and another backstage for the performers and crew.

Success On Stage (Audience Experience)	Success Backstage
• I am at the center of what they do • Product or service has a compelling story • Delivery lives up to the story • I have a great customer experience before, during, and after a sale • They delight in giving me a little more than	• Firm leadership sets a direction, casts a compelling vision and works with all levels to carry it out • Leadership demonstrates stability, integrity, approachability, agreeableness, collaboration, conscientiousness and openness

what I paid for • They respond to my needs • They listen to me • They continually improve my overall experience • They provide products and services in ways that reflect my values • I trust them to do the right thing even when it is not convenient to them. • There are opportunities for satisfaction and appreciation at all price levels. • Customer service, warranties, and replacements impress me	• Strong, clear core values • Shared passion for the firm's mission • Collegial environment • Hiring & retention of the best people through strong communication and teamwork competencies • Continual performance measurement • Collaborative attitudes • Opportunities to share ideas and opinions at all levels • Upward feedback mechanism for junior people to safely evaluate leadership • Room for different insights and problem-solving approaches • Meritocracy: if you deliver quality work consistently, you will have a long-term career with this firm, new and challenging opportunities, training, rewards and recognition • Zero tolerance for cut-throat politics

As a leader or someone with leadership ambitions, you must work tirelessly on executing successful strategies in both the front stage and backstage areas. Just as Tino was drawn to the circus life based on his experience as a customer and member of the audience, your first experience of your organization was probably similar to being part of the audience. Perhaps, you fell in love with the tiger as you watched it leap through rings of fire. When you joined the staff, you began to see reality or the "man behind the curtain." You learned that floors must be swept, sales targets must be met and IRS paperwork must be filed. There can be several steps that you need to take before you can dive in and do the work you're passionate about.

Have you been guilty of making Tino's first big mistake? When Tino reached out to touch the tiger, thinking he'd (literally) take the tiger by the tail, he brought his front stage viewpoint into the backstage world. Tino was ignorant of many facts, undereducated for the situation, failed to follow protocol, ignored the signals from others around him, and ended up looking like a fool. If luck had not been on his side that day, someone could have gotten hurt.

A business is a lot like that tiger. Everyone is dedicated to one purpose — creating a dazzling onstage spectacle that will wow the crowds. Everything they do every day, from pitching the tents to wielding a shovel, begins with that end in mind. All of it must be done with care and precision, lest the tiger get loose before the show even begins.

As Robert Cooper wrote, "We may not be interested in chaos but chaos is interested in us."[ii] The leader's job is not to keep chaos at bay with a whip and a chair, but to keep it from ever entering the ring.

When I was starting a new job at a large company, I was required to attend an orientation. The CEO looked at all of us in the room and said, "Every last one of you are rock stars. If that wasn't the case, you wouldn't be here. What you did before was enough to get you through the door. What you do now is a new chapter." That was a big revelation for me.

Successfully integrating into a thriving organization or leading one for that matter depends on everyone's understanding of best practices for both the front and backstage areas, and shared commitment to both short- and long-term plans. As Jack Welch said:

> You've got to eat while you dream. You've
> got to deliver on short-range commitments,
> while you develop a long-range strategy and
> vision and implement it. The success of doing
> both. Walking and chewing gum if you will.
> Getting it done in the short-range, and
> delivering a long-range plan, and
> executing on that.[iii]

Tino has to accept that what got him in the door is not going to get him any farther than that. He is going to have to pay attention, learn everything he can, and push himself harder than before. But hopefully, he will see what Leila and Raj already know about the Cirque Maravilla. As Steve Jobs said about the Beatles,

> They were four guys who kept each other's kind
> of negative tendencies in check. They balanced
> each other, and the total was greater than the
> sum of the parts. That's how I see business:
> Great things in business are never done by one
> person. They're done by a team of people.[iv].

3 - RUNNING THE SHOW

Tino emptied the last bucket of hay into the camels' feeding trough and leaned over the rail to pat a nearby neck. After six months of being on the road, he felt like he knew all of the animals better than they knew themselves. He liked working with Sergei, but often felt restless. As each day passed, there was less to learn and things became routine. Tino was now allowed to help Eileen and Sam rehearse the dogs each morning. That was a lot of fun and he looked forward to it. They even let him take on a small role in the act, moving props and holding up hoops. But it was clear that the couple still saw themselves as a duo and their routine didn't have room for a true third partner. At least my dog will be well-trained if I get one someday, he thought. Raj stopped by to talk with him sometimes, but there had been no invitation to join the tiger crew, not even for lunch. Tino was feeling stagnant and starting to wonder if he'd hit the canvas ceiling without hope for promotion.

Tino might have started feeling sorry for himself if he'd had a few minutes more to stand there and stare at the placidly chewing camels. But there was a sudden sound of truck tires on the gravel behind him and the sound of a window buzzing down. "Tino," shouted Leila, "Get behind the wheel here, will you? Joey's down with that flu we picked up in Albuquerque and I need a driver today." He didn't have to be asked twice. But you could have knocked him over with a feather when he saw "Lovely Leila Maravilla" was wearing a blouse, skirt, and blazer.

Quickly, Tino saw why running errands was a two-person job. It was a new town and Leila had to navigate while he drove. There were things to carry, packages to ship and supplies to be ordered. Tino was surprised by many of the stops that they made but was able to understand why the Ringmaster was dressed up like a middle school administrator. Leila filed paperwork with local officials and accepted instructions about local ordinances regarding space, traffic and trash disposal. They visited organizations with special groups. They went to schools and hospitals where "Circus Ambassadors" consisting mainly of clowns and dogs would make scheduled daytime visits in the near future. They also confirmed Port-o-John numbers and scheduled deliveries for that afternoon. He was even more surprised that most of these places were expecting their visit. "I start communicating with most of them by e-mail or phone when we're several weeks out.

Sometimes months in cities with strict code enforcement. If all of our elephants aren't in a row, the show can't go," explained Leila.

Even the expected tasks had unexpected protocols. When they dropped by the printer, Tino helped carry out a dozen heavy boxes to the truck. Tino asked, "Are we hanging paper all afternoon? Seems like a lot of posters!"

Leila shook her head and smiled. She said, "Those are for the rest of the season. This town's already hung." She pointed to a familiar image hanging in a shop window. "Joey comes a few days ahead to distribute them and work out promo ticket deals. If we wait until we're here to let them know we're coming, it's too late to build buzz."

They also dropped in on the local branch of the company bank, to discuss loan terms and an investment strategy for some of the recent revenue. Finally, she had him swing the truck into the lot of a coffee place. He sipped a latte — his first in months — and took notes while she interviewed candidates to take over as head cook at the start of the next season.

"You told me that the circus is a business," Tino said as he pointed the truck homeward, "I knew you weren't kidding. But, boy you weren't kidding! I had no idea how much marketing, paperwork, and human resources stuff you do. Most of this is stuff we covered in my classes, but I never expected to see it in an environment like ours."

She nodded and her face was serious. "This is our livelihood. Mine and yours. Everything has to be planned and executed carefully. It takes money to operate and a steady stream of revenue only results if the crowds keep coming. To them, it is an experience, a night's entertainment with the kids or a new girlfriend. But I have to look at it as a portfolio of products and services that we want them to buy. You want to get paid. I want to get people in those bleacher seats so I can keep the tent looking new, the tiger cages in good repair, plus pay you and everybody else."

"That's why my dad made me take 4 years away from the trapeze and go to college. At the time I resented it, all I wanted to do was fly, but I learned what I needed to know to bring this circus into the new millennium. And when my dad died, he knew his company was in good hands."

Tino nodded thoughtfully. He reflected on his first visit to the Cirque Maravilla, and how it had been motivated by seeing a combination of posters at his favorite hangouts and a feature in a local e-zine he followed. He thought about the crowds that showed up for each performance, and how everyone kept tabs on how many people filled those seats. If the tent was less than ¾ full, the mood at dinner was pretty somber. "It's a lot to keep up with," he agreed. "How many of the staff work on the daily marketing and operations with you?"

"Not enough." Leila grinned, "That's another reason why you're along today. Our season will be over soon, and we will be taking our standard three-month break. A lot of the crew and performers use the time to travel or see family. But how would you feel about coming to the home office and working on logistics for next season? You can put some of your degree skills to use. Plus Raj needs some help running auditions for new performers. He does that to help me out and because his family lives close, in New Jersey." Tino said he was interested and would let her know after he talked to his folks. His parents would be disappointed if he didn't come home, but he already knew he was in. She'd hooked him in as soon as she mentioned Raj.

If Tino thought learning to muck out pens and scrape out horse's hooves was hard, spending the winter at the office made that seem like a vacation. Every day was a whirlwind of activity. He made databases of local libraries and family centers to send promotional packets, created drip e-mail campaigns for the national fan club, compiled post-show surveys from the audience, and presented ideas on ways to save money and resources by moving materials to a digital format. He worked with Leila's mother, Ruby, on quarterly projections and budgets for the coming tour. They analyzed marketing techniques, and decided to abandon the moderately successful "Late Night" performances that had drawn adult audiences with a sensual theme. Ultimately, they felt it detracted from the company's "family-focused" reputation. Tino sat through hours of auditions with Raj, sorting resumes, watching jugglers and acrobats, scheduling call-backs and sending out rejection letters. He even helped create the "animal rotation" that decided which acts would perform at different stages of the season, to keep the animals from getting fatigued or stressed. This inspired him to pitch a new marketing strategy to Leila, connecting with affluent and educated parents who valued social justice and nature-friendly options for their kids.

By the beginning of March, Tino felt like he understood the circus in a whole new way. It now felt like a living, breathing thing to him and as he reflected on their conversation by the popcorn trailer, he thought that the circus must be to Leila what Raj's tigers were to him. She had the same understanding, constant watchfulness, and commitment to its health. She had to be vigilant or it would run amok and they would all suffer. She had to care for it attentively or it would sicken and die. The whole staff from cooks to performers were her crew.

Tino's day running errands with Leila had been the beginning of his real Big Top education. The months spent at the home office made him see how much the Cirque Maravilla had in common with the businesses he had studied in school. He came to realize how much responsibility the Martin family, especially Leila, carried. As the owner and Ringmaster, it fell to her to assemble and maintain the *right team; monitor the day-to-day with a big picture view; stay educated about all aspects of her market, her customer base, and the products and services she could successfully sell them; and promote her business and its aims to the outside world. These were the must-do activities of her world, and if she didn't do each one well, the Cirque Maravilla might not last another 75 days, let alone 75 years. He couldn't wait to get back on the road…but at the same time, he knew he'd never feel quite as carefree as he had that first season. He now felt just a little of the burden that Leila carried beneath that veneer of bravado and style that make up a Ringmaster's best disguise.*

🖋 🖋 🖋 🖋

A leader has to appreciate the difference between strategy and planning. Strategy is "what" while planning is "how." Strategy is composed of the ideas, the "stuff that has to be done" and the "never-ending quest for success." For Leila and others like her, successful strategizing depends on six key abilities:

1. To understand the company's culture and vision.
2. To know what the mission is and what objectives will be needed.
3. To formulate initiatives and tactics.

4. To execute pilots, demonstrations, and tests.

5. To institutionalize the biggest successes.

6. To respond to change.

Leila's months at home are dedicated studying all the available data about her performance from the past season, current market indicators on her tour route, changing behavior patterns for the audiences she hopes to attract and preparing the circus for its next tour. Her time on the road includes continual appraisal of new and changing factors. How will she know how many posters to order and what community organizations might enjoy a visit from her circus ambassadors if she does not look at past performance? Doing this work gives her a broad base of knowledge that she shares with her administrative team. The team uses this knowledge make specific decisions about who to hire, where to go, how to spend money, who to send advertising, and host of other decisions. Planning places strategy within a specific time and framework. It helps define who will be involved and what processes are necessary to achieve desired results. Planning must be based on the best information available about your environment and customers. Planning materializes in the form of concrete action steps that you and your team execute.

There are six key steps in planning:

1. Identify the necessary tasks
2. Identify the needed roles
3. Train your people to perform required tasks
4. Identify needs such as budget, space, etc.
5. Identify risks
6. Identify value to customer

Of course, strategy development and planning means absolutely nothing if your organization can't successfully perform in the marketplace. Could the circus survive without the crowds? Leila's years of experience have taught her otherwise, and now Tino knew it too. The marketplace will continue to be the best validator of whether business plans, products, and services are what the customers need, when they need it, and at a price they are willing to pay. Your tiger is not like the ones in the jungle. If no one is watching, he will starve.

All strategies and plans are subject to continual cycles of assessment and modification. Proper execution depends on getting things in the right order: plan, do, check, and react. Initial execution is the "do" part; leadership should always follow up with assessment and reaction. Repeat what works well and fix what doesn't. This requires clearly defined performance standards for people, for plans, and for products or services.

- What is "success?" What is "health" for your tiger?
  - o The evidence should be measurable: How many tickets have been sold? How many ice cream cones? How many visitors rated their experience as "very satisfactory" or above?

- Is the organization hitting the benchmarks that have been set?
  - o Leila and Ruby consistently monitor sales/profitability/performance numbers and review them frequently. They may decide to cut a city from the next season, or add nights there, depending on how well the circus has done in the past.
  - o They monitor customer response and satisfaction, too. It is important to note

whether audiences are increasing or decreasing at a given stop. Are their current customers buying tickets at previous levels, bringing new people with them, or skipping the show this year? Are they articulating positive responses to interactions with your organization?

Anything that doesn't work must be modified or abandoned. If remediation is possible, determine what can be fixed, find the best solution, and implement it. If money can be saved in the bigger cities by abandoning posters in favor of digital ads in the local media, or if younger parents prefer to receive information via social media, then the administrative team is responsible of carrying out those changes. When something (project, methodology or individual member) is not working out, you must also be willing to cut it, as Cirque Maravilla did with the "adults only" shows that were diluting its customer base.

All the best strategy and planning will be ineffective if you do not have the right people to execute them. Both strategy and planning depend on the ability of the organization's people to bring them to life. Tino is one of the many people that Leila counts on. She must also trust that Joey is efficient and effective as the show's advance man and that Ed Naeglin will see the tents are properly constructed and safe. Leila has to communicate well with the clowns so that they will strike the right tone when they visit a local hospital and that Rita's people will keep the horses in line backstage. She's also got to supervise the cooks so that they serve meals on time and in accordance with health codes. Leila's also in charge of managing Raj and his crew so they won't let the cats escape into the crowd. The success of the circus is tied to its performance and its performance in turn, is tied to a number of individual actions and smoothly running processes. If any one person slacks off or can't perform to the expected standard, the whole circus may suffer.

The following chapters demonstrate the importance of getting the whole team involved in strategy, planning, and execution. As Leila and Raj both know, there are five leadership activities that should never be neglected or left to chance:

1. Know the team members' skills and limitations.

2. Monitor spheres of influence and interpersonal dynamics.

3. Delegate the right tasks to the right people at the right time.

4. Motivate and empower them with a consistent schedule of feedback and reinforcement, including rewards, discipline, and help.

5. Assess, assess, assess.

These are the things that a would-be tiger tamer like Tino needs to know before he is ready to take on the challenge of taming a tiger on his own.

4 - THE RUNNING CREW

The start of the spring tour was a blast! Everyone was glad to be back on the road. The crowds were responsive after the winter's entertainment lull and Tino enjoyed the challenge of his new responsibilities. There were some small kinks to work out, like when Rita broke her ankle with a mistimed jump, but everyone was pitching in to keep the show going. Tino was happy that every afternoon he had permission to spend two hours observing the tiger crew. At the start of the season, Raj instructed him to sit out of the way and take notes on everything that he noticed about their work. Twice a week, after the last show of the day, they would sit down together to discuss what he'd seen.

At first, he had focused only on what the tigers were doing, trying to make connections to what he'd read in Raj's copy of Tiger Anatomy and Training. Then one evening the older man stopped him mid-sentence and asked, "Tino, how many people were working the cage during tonight's show?" Embarrassed, he admitted he didn't know. "Well, starting tomorrow, you need to pay more attention to what the humans are doing. That's what counts."

Tino took that advice to heart. He began to see many new and important details, like the fact that there were five people on the crew, but never more than two in the cage. He saw how they worked in pairs during performances: moving panels in the cages to let the animals in or out, opening portals to place props, and moving stands as unobtrusively as possible. In daylight they worked the tigers with things that looked like enormous cat toys: shredded blankets on ropes, a ball dangling from a pole. They fed them small tidbits of meat, but never wiped their hands off on their clothes. They wrestled, jumped, and played catch with the beasts, but never looked away for more than a few seconds. He saw that Francine walked through the cage every day, testing the fasteners and inspecting the welds. Tino weighed, measured and inspected the meat closely. Then he checked the water in their pool every day using a little testing kit and ordered supplies when things got low.

Early on, Raj explained the assignment of tasks. He told Tino, "Jamie and Josh make sure the props and toys are all safe and in good repair. We don't want one of the cats getting a cut paw. Hiro monitors nutrition and environmental conditions, and he works with

Sergei an anything else connected to their health. Francine has engineering training, so she leads the build and teardown on all the enclosures and she coordinates with Ed when something needs repair or replacing. Dan's got a degree in animal behavior, and comes from a circus family. So he coordinates with me on exercise and training for all three cats; he reports if they are agitated or listless, and makes sure everyone's safe when we rehearse or have play time for them. Everyone takes a turn on waste clean-up and disposal, cleaning our trailers, and running errands. We've been a little short staffed since Patrick left a few months ago, but everyone has picked up the slack."

"What happened to him?" asked Tino, wondering why anyone would ever leave this crew.

Raj shook his head, "Never really fit in. He resented having clean up duty and didn't quite hustle as hard as the others felt he should. No one ever bad-mouthed him, but it was clear they felt he was a slacker. I eventually suggested he'd be happier with Ed's crew, and he put in for a transfer. I think he's left the circus altogether, now."

Tino began to observe how Raj interacted with his team. The Tamer didn't watch his crew's every move - he was too busy watching the tigers. But he didn't have to - they were always right where they were supposed to be, doing what they'd been assigned to do. Tino could see that they were all really good, really experienced, and really confident. When they sat together at meals or in meetings, Raj listened to what they said. He asked their opinions on the animals, the equipment, or the performance. He shared personal stories and asked them about themselves, without prying or getting too far off-topic. If a show went well, he ended the night with simple, measured words of praise. If someone made a mistake, he gave them a chance to offer a plan for correction before making suggestions himself. He never yelled unlike Dan, who tended to get pretty testy if he felt things weren't going well. Tino was often amazed at how patient Raj was with Dan's temper, quietly reining him in when necessary. I'd read that guy the riot act, if it were me! He often thought. But he saw the value of Raj's calm, respectful approach and respected Raj for it.

After a few weeks, Raj asked Tino, "Do you understand what everyone does during the show?"

The would-be tamer had learned to be cautious and replied, "I think I'm starting to get it. You keep the audience's attention on you, and direct the tigers in the routine. Francine stands behind you and cues the changes of equipment. Dan handles the props in the ring, and helps you watch in case someone gets irritable, like Pasha did last night. He signals Josh and Jamie, who move the panels quickly, and coaxes the tiger off-stage, where Hiro gets them into a crate and soothes them. When the act is done, the four of you get the cats back to their quiet enclosure as quick as possible while Josh and Jamie help break down the set and move it." He stopped and looked to Raj for approval.

Raj nodded and continued, "And why do we coordinate that closely?"

"Because it has to look seamless to the audience. The cats need to do everything you say as soon as you say it, and even if they look fierce, you want them to think it's play time. If they get upset for any reason, which could ruin the whole act or someone could get injured."

"Right," agreed Raj, "and that's also why I select crew members based on temperament as well as skills. You've got to be calm and laid back, but alert, to work with these animals. They don't like high-strung or noisy people." Seeing Tino's expression, he grinned. "Hey, the crew might snipe around the table sometimes. But they've all got to be totally collected in the ring. And they trust each other. They let go of the little stuff."

"I've been meaning to ask," said Tino, a little tentatively, "What's the protocol if something goes really wrong, if one of the tigers gets aggressive or startled?"

Raj smiled, "Join us for lunch tomorrow, and then we'll show you."

🐾 🐾 🐾 🐾

Tino's observations of the tiger crew's work have given him some important insights about the nature of high performance teams. The team had Raj as leader, and each crew member had a clear sense of the team's common purpose and goals. Looking around at the rest of the circus, Tino could see that this was equally true for other crews from the acrobats to the tent-assembly guys. Each group had a very clear purpose, responsibilities to perform, and each person had to know their individual role in that process.

Raj knew every detail of what went into his act and how to define each role on his crew. The tigers needed daily care, feeding, exercise, and training. Raj knew that he needed people with specialized skills in exotic animal welfare. He also needed help in managing the animals, working the crowd, and maintaining safety. Raj needed someone who could assertively direct the efforts of both people and cats. The team also needed good equipment that won't fail and individuals with technical and engineering expertise to operate them. With those things in mind, he has carefully chosen a group of people who can help him accomplish his goals and been explicit with each of them about what to do.

Tino also has a new appreciation for the interpersonal dynamics of a team and for the impact of personality on job performance. He had never thought about temperament as a factor in tiger taming, but clearly the work can be stressful and dangerous. Naturally it requires a cool head, attentiveness, and quick thinking. Healthy teams depend on the right mix of disposition or at least on managing limitations. Thinking back to his old college volunteer work, he remembers how the right players made work easier, but conflict could totally wreck a good plan. Back then it was annoying, but in a work environment like this, it could be disastrous. Clearly, Patrick had the right skills or he never would have been invited to join the tiger crew, but his poor attitude and distaste for menial tasks made it impossible for him to bond with the others. And Dan might be really great with the animals—no one would deny it—but his harsh and impatient criticism clearly has an impact on morale, even if the others take it in stride.

Leaders like Raj and Leila need a lot more than good stage presence to succeed. They depend on high performance teams—teams they must build and maintain. While you can't always control who is present when you join an organization, ultimately, you get the crew you make for yourself. That's why your most essential tasks will always include:

1. Recruiting the right people: Do they have the needed skills or can they master them quickly? Are their personalities suited to the work that they must do?

2. Minimizing politics and maintaining a pleasant atmosphere: Hey, we don't live in Munchkinland. Personal conflicts arise. You must encourage people to remain polite and positive, and resolve or let go of resentment.

3. Creating an environment that is fun or at least pleasant, for the team: No one should dread coming into the office. You don't have to provide bean bag chairs and pinball, but make sure the space is comfortable, and people have what they need to be productive. Make sure good people have the opportunity to grow and get rewarded.

4. Modeling integrity and good behavior or decision-making yourself: Your employees will follow your lead in terms of behavior.

5. Making sure everyone constantly understands mission and shares vision: If even one person messes

up, gets distracted, or stops caring, you could get eaten by your tiger.

Tino has already had the opportunity to observe the positive results of a strong leadership style. He sees that both Leila and Raj engage in behaviors that empower a team. The members have equity and permission to express their own thoughts and ideas. They have responsibility and space to work without constant supervision (which is just as essential for both a ringmaster and tiger tamer to do their own jobs). Those who do well receive encouragement, flexibility, and the opportunity for growth. In fact, he's very much hoping to benefit from that himself in the near future. From Raj, Tino learned firsthand how problematic it can be to have a low performer on board or someone who does not fit into the company culture. While Tino's awareness of company teams and culture has grown, he is now stepping into the reality of hiring and maintaining teams. He's about to learn the real nuances of on-boarding and off-boarding team members as well as deal with the daily operational challenges necessary to create and sustain a high performance team.

5 - GETTING INTO THE ACT

Watching the tiger crew work from a safe distance was one thing - spending all day with them was quite another. Tino had learned enough to realize that he probably would not be able to pick up a chair and a whip on the first day. But he at least he thought he'd get to pet one of the cats before two months had passed. Wrong. Instead he learned to help assemble and disassemble the cage and enclosures. His primary job was to assist Jamie and Josh in quick construction and teardown of the metal structures during each show. Not quite the glamorous role he had imagined for himself on that night so many months before.

He actually enjoyed spending his days with Raj's team, though it took him some time to fit in. Josh and Jamie were immediately welcoming. The brothers were funny and unpretentious. Hiro was quiet, but glad to answer Tino's questions and very patient in explaining new information. Francine ignored him completely, except when she was giving him directions; clearly she expected he would flake out like Patrick had done, but he thought he could win her trust with hustle and a good attitude. When his turn for laundry came, he made sure to return her clothes freshly pressed and folded, and she warmed up considerably. Dan was another story. Clearly he had not forgotten the "Tiger cologne" incident and was just waiting for Tino to screw up. He didn't say anything directly because that would question Raj's judgment in bringing Tino in, but he took every opportunity to criticize or find fault. Tino didn't like it, but he kept his own temper in check. However, other crew members began to step in, helping Tino before he made a mistake, patting him on the back after Dan walked away, or even occasionally diffusing Dan's temper before a real argument ignited.

Raj didn't let him enter the enclosure for a long time, explaining that the big cats didn't like new and unexpected things. He was allowed to move around the perimeter, help shift equipment when the tigers weren't inside, and assist with food and water. All of this gave the animals time to adjust to his presence from a distance, especially his smell. Eventually he was allowed to stand inside and observe while Francine and Dan exercised the cats, then to toss them an occasional treat, and finally to help Raj with grooming. Tino knew that getting to play or perform with the tigers was still a long way off however and might even take years.

Tino's interest might have waned with such delays in gratification if Raj had not included Tino in practically every other aspect of caring for the tigers. Tino attended the tiger crew meetings, was assigned daily chores, ate with the crew, and had a bunk in their trailers. Except for the few hours a week that he spent on administrative tasks for Leila, Tino was with the tiger crew full time.

Once again, what he learned really surprised him. In addition to the parts of the job that involved direct care and interaction with the tigers, the team spent time every day on the whole act and its place in the circus. They discussed costumes, rehearsed poses and gestures, and coordinated with the band on new music. Tino learned the reason why Josh, Jamie, and Hiro wore plain grey coveralls while Raj, Francine, and Dan wore red and black—it was all about calling the audience's attention to the right things. They went over Leila's information on each town and tweaked the act depending on the demographic and local factors. The team was always aware of how the whole circus was doing in terms of marketing and revenue. They brainstormed ideas for merchandise connected to the act, making occasional changes based on Leila's sales numbers. They also reviewed the tigers' health and recent behavior, constantly assessing their stress levels and fitness for the shows. If a tiger seemed out of sorts, it did not go on stage that night.

There were regular skills assessments. Josh, Jamie, and Tino verbally walked through enclosure assembly steps every day, using musical cues to get the timing just right. Once a week there was an emergency drill, using a large dummy tiger, where the crew rehearsed a response to any angry or violent behavior. While Hiro was in charge of the tranquilizer gun that was always kept at hand, every crew member was expected to practice marksmanship and be ready to fire a dart that would hit a rogue cat and put them out of commission. They also practiced first aid and transport techniques for a serious injury. Raj would frequently ask crew members questions on tiger behavior, crew protocol, and circus policies. They were expected to answer quickly and correctly; any mistakes meant remedial reading and writing a report. A mistake during rehearsal or performance meant even closer scrutiny and a formal correction plan, though team members were generally quick to support and encourage each other if something went wrong. It was clear that they all understood the stakes, but that everyone understood human error, too.

Tino also began to consider other questions and comments that Raj would make. The tamer was subtly and constantly assessing his crew, monitoring their satisfaction and giving them additional responsibilities and autonomy if he was pleased with their performance. Sometimes he sent Francine over to help Ed with a difficult engineering problem, or let Hiro assist Sergei with nutrition plans for other animals. If Dan asked to visit a university expert in a town where they were stopped, Raj gave his blessing. No one felt bored or under-valued, and they were all encouraged to seek new information on a variety of topics—from tiger maintenance to circus finance—that they could share with the group.

Within a few weeks, Tino felt much more at home and he could tell that the team was confident that he would be more than "another Patrick." He also understood how the crew operated and how it served the circus's mission. It struck him one night as he drifted to sleep in his bunk, listening to the hum of the trailers moving down the road, while they might have been surprised to learn it, Tino was living what many of his old business professors would have called "operational excellence."

🖋 🖋 🖋 🖋

You might be wondering what is operational excellence and how Tino is doing it. Operational excellence starts with proper on boarding - organizational members need to know and understand the company. That process should begin even before official hires are made, with educating applicants. Once new people are brought in, they should quickly master the core knowledge:

- What are our values?

- Who are our customers?

- What are standard policies and procedures?
- What are the practical things every employee is going to need to know to do?
- What are the consequences of neglect and/or errors in executing?

Tino's education started the day Leila sized him up in her office, and his first days with the circus. He had quickly learned that everyone from the cooking crew to jugglers to acrobats could repeat the company's mission, had a crystal clear understanding of the rules and standards, shared its values, and acted appropriately for the culture. In a way, it was a cohesive close-knit community that large organizations only dreamed about having and executing well.

Now that Tino had become part of a mission-critical, high performance team, he began the specialized on-boarding process designed for the tiger crew. His professional development from certification to advanced training, professionalism, and competencies would now be managed within that environment.

Operational excellence allows strategies to be deployed successfully, and should always be a goal for performance management, process, and high performance teams. For a methodology or practice to be considered "excellent," it must advance the goals of the organization and it must be sustainable.

Consistent operational excellence has a number of benefits. These include the characteristics that Tino noticed are features of his team:

- There are opportunities for individuals and groups to grow and improve
- Employees are happy, empowered, and productive
- Product or service gets to market efficiently
- Chances for ROI are maximized
- Remarkable results are achieved in short term and over the long range.

Tino has also been fortunate to have joined an organization that clearly values operational excellence and has a clear understanding of how to create it. He has not had to see the consequences of operational mediocrity or failure. Leaders like Leila and Raj must know what to look out for. When operations do not run efficiently or mindfully:

- Effort is internally directed, and expended on making up for lack of organization instead of on expansion (outwardly directed)
- Time and effort get wasted
- Costs go up
- Team members are unhappy and perform below standard
- Product/service may be delayed or inadequate (problems, flaws, dated, etc.)
- Windows of opportunity are missed
- Revenue is lost
- Company gets left behind, perhaps leading to organizational demise.

Whether he understands the implications or not, Tino is enjoying a unique opportunity. He is able to observe a strong model for how to achieve sustained operational excellence.

Both Raj and Leila focus on core competencies in their areas of immediate influence. What must we do well to achieve? What do we already do well that we can maintain? Where do we need to improve? Having relevant up-to-date information and using it well is key on all levels.

Team members all understand the "life cycle" of responsibilities for their team. They also get exposure to the major areas of responsibility for other parts of the organization. Ideally, they should do rotations so that they understand how to support the team in different ways. This has the added benefit of creating redundancy in case of emergency.

Teams and stakeholders communicate and coordinate across the organization.

The team has an external as well as internal focus. They are well-informed not only about the organization, but the market, target market, technology and innovation, etc. An educated team has a sense of the organization's place in the "big picture" and can help respond to it.

At this point, Tino's eyes are really open to what it means to be backstage at the "Greatest Show on Earth." He understands the complexity of day-to-day operations for the organization and sees the necessity of operational excellence on both the micro level (his new team) and the macro level (the circus as a whole). Perhaps it is time for him and us to direct our attention to the center ring and talk about our reason for performing or the one aspect that motivates everything else in the circus or your business: the Audience.

6 - "LADIES AND GENTLEMEN, CHILDREN OF ALL AGES": FINDING AND KEEPING AN AUDIENCE

The circus always anticipated the early summer leg of their tour. Kids were out of school and the evening weather in most places was mild, so the crowds came out in droves. The mood of the whole organization had been upbeat and spirited; the clowns celebrated by pulling small practical jokes on anyone who wasn't watching their back, and even Rita occasionally smiled. May and June were fantastic, and they anticipated traveling the mountain states as a way to avoid the July heat of the South. Then suddenly, Tino noticed a change. As the circus crew crossed the border into Colorado, a new tension filled the air overnight. Performers and crew members alike were on edge, and getting increasingly nervous as they got closer to the next big regional stop.

After a week of watching twitchy behavior and hearing nervous references to the town in question, Tino finally looked at Leila over a stack of publicity photos and asked, "What gives?"

She sighed, "This town used to be a big money-maker for us. But for the last two years we have had some trouble. There's an animal rights group with big membership in this state, and they have staged some disruptive protests during our visits. The staff gets pretty nervous, and there's a lot of talk about doing this town without any of the animals, or even taking it off our route altogether. But I'm not ready to give up. We have worked hard to build and maintain a fan base here, families who have come to see us for years."

For a moment, Tino was too stunned to speak. It wasn't the protests themselves. He had been to zoos and animal parks where activists regularly camped out with signs, and he knew some people had strong opinions on animals that couldn't easily be swayed. It was Leila's tone of frustration and doubt. He had seen her analyze demographic charts and entertainment trends, had helped her work on ad campaigns that emphasized Cirque Maravilla's unique qualities. He had marveled over her uncanny ability to pick the merchandise options that would sell best, and he watched her work the crowd every night. He knew she knew how to sell her show. So why was she feeling so intimidated now?

"Well, I don't want to meddle in things that are above my pay grade," he said slowly, *"But I've helped out a few times in dealing with disgruntled customers. We have good policies there. You taught me how to manage complaints, how to diffuse a loud or angry patron, and when to offer a refund or just show them the gate. The marketing crew is really good at handling negative reviews with attractive publicity - plus the performers are always willing to make changes if something doesn't play well."*

"Yeah," sighed Leila, *"But those techniques don't really work with protestors like these folks."*

"Still, I remember going over this town with Ruby. They are still a perfect fit for us in many ways. There are lots of families with kids in the right age range. They like to spend money on entertainment. There are two just two other outfits that come through — one other circus and the other a big carnival, if I remember right."

Leila nodded, *"But our approach is very different from theirs. Sometimes I send Joey or one of the others to see those shows, if their route passes close to ours. So we have a clear picture of where things are similar and what makes us distinctive. In fact, I know one of them recently got in trouble with the ASPCA for their animal care practices."*

"So the market isn't saturated, and it may be that these protesters are keeping other competition at bay," Tino replied. He

sighed, thinking hard and rubbing his eyes. And then, Leila's favorite inspirational quote echoed in his head. He knew it by heart now, but he asked, "Leila, what's that saying you like...the one about selling the sizzle instead of the steak?"

"No. Some people say, 'Sell the sizzle and not the steak.' But I like what Bob Allen says, 'Sell the sizzle BUT DELIVER THE STEAK! AND the salad AND the hors d'oeuvres AND the dessert AND the after-dinner drink, AND the limo ride to and from the restaurant.'" That's what we try to do."

Tino sat up straight. "Well, I think that applies here, too. When I first got here, all I could think about was the applause, getting my chance to get in front of a crowd and impressing them. But in the last year I've learned a lot about how much you have to do to get them in the tent. And I'm starting to see how intentional Raj and the others are about creating a spectacle they'll respond to. So, couldn't we apply that same technique in this case? I had a college professor who used to really drill us about how important it is now for customers to see that your brand's values match theirs. And we already have some permission-based marketing in place with our e-mail list and social media, right?"

"True," Leila agreed, looking intrigued. "We do have a database for this city, and we just sent out the first 'Get ready for the circus!' e-mail yesterday. I'm all ears."

"Well, couldn't we launch an education campaign, show them how we treat our animals, how much we contribute to welfare and conservation organizations like Annabeth's elephant park? Does this town even know that the elephants don't join us here because the travel is too stressful for them to come this far?"

"No, they don't," replied Leila, "and we could teach them that. Plus, the demographics show that the population is educated. I could give a few more facts about some of the animals, like the tigers, during the act. We could create a fun worksheet to give parents, and they could fill it in with their kids as they watch!"

"Oh, and they could put in the answers on our website when they get home! We could send them a little prize like a circus sticker as a reward, which would allow us to collect some more social media fans!" Now they were both excited about the prospects.

By the time the trucks pulled into the fairground in the town in question, the whole organization was ready. Leila had contacted a popular television reporter, and invited her to bring her kid and her camera crew for a personal lesson on how to care for the horses. Stickers were added to the posters, displaying the logos of the animal charities the circus supported. E-mail and social media blasts included a short essay on Annabeth's elephant sanctuary, with links to YouTube videos and the website for the sanctuary itself. During their stay, the camels and a few of the dogs—all selected for patience and temperament—were brought out in front of the tent every evening so patrons could have a picture taken with them. Everyone also had clear instructions that if the media asked about the protestors, they were to:

a) express admiration for the group's dedication to animals,

b) stress that animal care and conservation was a core value for Cirque Maravilla,

c) extend an invitation to the group to attend a performance as special guests.

While none of the protestors took advantage of the offer, it was clear that the town's concerns quieted down. The media sang the circus's praise for both an entertaining spectacle and a focus on animal welfare. Many families completed the worksheet and claimed their special tiger sticker, which Ruby sent by mail (after adding the names to the database). The whole staff expressed a sense of relief, happy that their proactive approach had kept them out of harm's way.

Tino was just happy that he'd helped keep the tigers safe.

🐾 🐾 🐾 🐾

Winning an audience is work. After you get them to show up, you have to keep them coming back. If you are in a leadership position in any organization, or you aspire to be, then I am guessing you already know that. The trick is in: a) getting your whole team/organization to be equally clear on this priority and invested in making it happen, and b) to find the specific methodology that will help your unique business get it done.

To successfully market your product or service, you have to know it better than you know yourself. Know your strengths, your differentiators, uniqueness, and competitive edge. Know your offering inside and out. In your advertising and publicity, be aware that most people are going to want the "highlights," so perfect your "elevator pitch" and use it consistently across all media. You should be able to write a dissertation on it, too. There will be potential clients, partners, or investors who want detailed information before they commit. Make sure it is accessible, and make double-sure that everyone in the organization is educated on it.

It is equally important to know what else is out there. What are the potential options for buyers? What choices do they have in terms of a solution for their pain or problem? There's no need to run down the competition, which can backfire and make you look petty or envious.

It's imperative that you recognize your strengths and have awareness, Know your unique value. Know your competition. Know the difference. Just explain why you use your methods. Focus on proving to the potential buyer what they stand to gain from choosing you.

As Tino has learned from working in the home office with Ruby, you have to start with researching your potential client. Do your demographic homework so you can design your product or service to fill a real need, and confirm that the people best suited for your offering can and will engage with it. In addition, you have to build excitement; you have to be intentional about advertising, attracting solid leads, and closing. The key to creating that enthusiasm and sustaining your audience's interest involves the following:

1. Have a compelling story
2. Tell it well
3. Disseminate it on the right channels
4. Monitor what works and what doesn't, then make changes
5. Partner with organizations that can do things you can't. If you use outsourcing or collaboration for other things from building your product to managing

your books, etc., why would you not do the same for your marketing? Leverage the media, publicity firms, or any other group that has skills you can use.

The first rule of marketing is to treat the customer with the same respect and interest that you would want to receive. It is absolutely critical that you should:

- Get to know them. Never neglect your research on the target market
- Provide what they want/need.
- Give them their money's worth. Get all teams/team members invested in delivering great experience.
  - As you monetize your product/service offerings, be sure customers at all levels are happy and satisfied. The current climate encourages lots of 'tiers' of service in order to maximize profit. This is fine. Leila and her crew have various packages and VIP offers for patrons to enhance their entertainment experience. Let your customers choose the level of service they want to pay for, and that

they feel good about it. But make sure that no one leaves feeling like economy travelers on a second-rate airline.

- Engage in open communication and response to feedback (Social media can be great for this).

As a leader, you should never allow your team or organization to neglect these priorities. They should be part of your institutional culture.

The key to doing these things successfully is to adapt quickly. Rather than reacting to the protestors when confronted by them, Leila and her staff proactively prepared for the situation. They already had solid execution on their marketing strategy: knowing who was most likely to come to the show, contacting potential buyers in advance. They had sound policies for dealing with problems and complaints, which help them diffuse negative publicity and customer dissatisfaction. In the end, it was these best practices, together with a little creative thinking, that allowed them to be adaptable in the face of a new challenge.

7 - BRAND TO BEAT THE BAND

The protestor situation had a happy ending as far as the circus folk were concerned. Everyone began to refer to it as "The Colorado Plan." The episode however got Tino thinking. All of the staff understood that making a profit was important, but it didn't seem like everyone really got how you did that. Clearly, Leila had a vision and her team developed a strategy to make it happen, but did guys like Connor the Juggler or Ed Naeglin get it? What about Rita or the clowns? The more he watched, the more convinced Tino became that most of the crew and performers were really only interested in doing their own specific jobs. They were happy leaving the big picture stuff to someone else. But Raj was different. Tino took a few days to work up some courage and finally knocked on Raj's trailer door during the afternoon rest period.

As they sat down together, Tino got straight to the point. He said, "I learned a lot about marketing while I was at the home office this winter, but that whole deal with the protestors was something new. It really shook up the organization."

Raj nodded, "But you did great work. Leila tells me that you played a big part in helping us turn that around."

Shrugging modestly, Tino went on. "I guess so. But it made me see that most of the people working here don't really get stuff like marketing or public relations. I mean, they know how to work an audience, but it stops there. You're different, though. I've been paying more attention lately. I can't think of a better way to say it, but I'm starting to see that you really put effort into making your act its own brand." Seeing Raj smile and nod like he was both surprised and pleased was encouraging. So he took a deep breath and said, "Can you teach me how you do it?"

"Why don't you start by telling me what you've observed?" replied Raj.

"Some of it's pretty obvious. You've got your costume, and the coordinating ones for Dan and Francine. You all keep yourselves really fit, and have a consistent way of presenting yourself in the ring, with carefully timed gestures and poses. You plan the musical score with the band so that it matches the pace of the act, and has a kind of Bollywood-meets-hip hop flavor. All of the materials paint you as the descendent of royalty from India—which is a total lie, because your family lives in Jersey!"

"Well, I was born in South Orange, that's true," laughed Raj, "But my parents are from India. I found out early on in my career that nobody is impressed with an animal trainer who was raised by computer programmers. There's not a lot of glam or glitz in that, and a circus is all about exotic spectacle. So, I grew an impressive mustache and created 'Rajah,' who has a much more romantic family history than my own. Later, Leila helped me work it up into a story that sounded really epic. The crowds expect a little storytelling and embellishment. It's all in good fun, and I never use the character offstage."

"So, how else do you promote your image? How much is it like the stuff I've read about brand management?"

"Brand management is exactly what it is, Tino. My brand is an offshoot of and support for the Cirque Maravilla's brand. You already know how Leila and Ruby position us as a traditional circus for modern families—something authentic and reminiscent of old times, but with some 21st century technology and ideas thrown in. Everything reflects that: the posters, all of our publicity images, the look of the tents, sets, and costumes, the music. And thanks to you, we're doing more to emphasize how conservation- and earth-friendly we are. "

He held up a hand and raised one finger. "It starts with catching the public's eye and attracting their attention. We use our advertising and public appearances for that." Holding up a second finger, he went on, "The design of the text and the layout of the grounds, the sets and the costumes are all intended to be visually appealing and memorable. All of the acts are allowed to design their own stuff, but they understand it is important that the final product needs to be consistent and coordinated. So we brought in a design expert to help us with colors, patterns, and shapes. The clowns nearly rioted over that at first; they're not used to having to think about anything but their own stunts. But eventually they came around. It was that designer's idea to put me and the tiger crew in the red and black leather, which are apparently colors that inspire excitement and danger in the audience's mind. He suggested the light grey that you, Josh, and Jamie all wear, so you are less visible during the transitions. And he created that special backdrop we use. It makes the pattern of the tigers' skin really stand out."

"That's awesome," interrupted Tino, "and I see why that's important. But what I really mean is where did you go from there? What do you do to build a relationship with them?"

"I'm getting there," Raj chuckled, holding up a third finger. "Most of the acts emphasize closeness with the audience. Leila wants the kids to feel like the performers know each of them is out there. And the parents are encouraged to get a feeling of innocence, like they've brought their children into a simpler time. Even the lighting is designed to look old-fashioned, even though it is pretty hi-tech. So everything is designed to feel inviting, personal, and kind of retro. That works to our advantage, too, because the vintage thing is big with young adults and lets us connect with them."

He paused for a breath, and then went on, "But we decided that the tiger act needed to be a little different. Thanks to our e-mail campaigns and our clown ambassadors, most of them walk through the door with some guidelines on circus etiquette. We can let them pet the camels, interact with the dogs, stand with the elephants. But they can't get anywhere near the tigers. So my act is intended to inspire a sense of mystery. I'm elusive, always a bit beyond their grasp. Did you know I have my own newsletter for the circus fans?" Tino shook his head. "It's the most direct connection I have with them. I share news about the circus and facts on the animals. There are serialized stories about the tigers, which Francine writes. She's really good, actually. My character is like a guru or a wise man who is benevolent but a little distant. The audience loves it. We are close enough that they can get a good view, but always just out of reach. Nothing could create more curiosity and desire!"

At this point, Tino thought he was starting to catch on. "Yeah. I can see how the tent and grounds are set up to create that intimacy, but the tiger enclosure isn't approachable. The merchandise all matches the color schemes and themes, and the toys all reflect something they see *in the different acts. Choosing to sell the little tiger models instead of stuffed toys, is that part of your brand strategy?"*

"Absolutely!" Raj grinned. "We don't trivialize the tigers. Our audiences see them for what they are: wild animals. And they eat it up."

Suddenly, Tino realized why the Colorado plan had worked so well - it aligned well with the circus's existing brand. They already had an excellent reputation as solid family entertainment with an appealing look and feel that audiences enjoyed. The public had a favorable opinion of them and was ready to believe the best as long as the circus made an effort to show that it was responsible and caring as well as a fun experience. The audience had been primed to expect a certain relationship with the performers and animals. The care that Cirque Maravilla had taken to build that relationship then allowed the crew to meet the potential crisis proactively and turn it into an advantage.

🐾 🐾 🐾 🐾

Your brand is the unique personality of your organization, the character of its products and services, what makes it recognizable and different from all others. Your brand is your character, but it more complex than that. Branding is relationship-building or creating a connection between you organization and your customer. That sense of connection and that bond, is what will distinguish you from your competition in their minds and cultivate a sense of loyalty to your products and services.

Building a brand identity requires focused, intentional work. You might luck into a good idea, but a whole brand never comes together by accident. The best branding is based around a strong, compelling idea. Once that is in place, a strategy must be formulated and executed. There is an information technology premise that works equally well for thinking about branding. It's called the "Unified Theory of Acceptance."

- **Contact.** The first phase is initial contact. The public encounters something new.
- **Awareness.** In the second phase, you create awareness. The audience is asked to pay attention to this new thing, to acknowledge it.
- **Understanding.** The third phase requires the creation of understanding. The audience must learn more about the thing in question. They need to

know how it works, what its uses are.

- **Positive Perception**. Now that the public knows about your brand, they must not feel concern, suspicion, or fear. They need to believe that this new idea or entity is a good thing.

- **Experimentation**. Curiosity comes into play. People start to wonder, "What else could be done with this? How can I use it? Will it do something to make my life better or more interesting?

- **Adoption**. The audience is now accustomed to the idea or entity. They like it (or at least see the necessity of it), and integrate it into the fabric of their lives.

I've also added two more steps to this process:

- **Institutionalization**. The idea or entity is thoroughly incorporated into the culture of your target market.

- **Globalization**. The idea or entity spreads beyond its original borders and into new territory.

Your brand can become one of your organization's best assets. It creates your reputation and relationship and the Cirque Maravilla relies on that fact. Having an attractive, high profile brand helps them to build anticipation in their target market for each of the stops on their tour. It brings in repeat business as families return year after year, and draws new customers who want to see what everyone's raving about.

The right blends of traditional and social media marketing are essential for developing and maintaining the relationship between your audience and your brand. Leila and Raj understand that the relationship does not begin and end at the point of purchase, but must be continually nurtured. Fortunately, technology and social media have greatly expanded their ability to do that. They have multiple channels to stay in touch, to remind audiences who they are and carry on a conversation. Potential customers can visit their website to find information on the organization and its activities; Flickr and Twitter provide a means of interacting regularly and directly; e-mail campaigns alert fans about upcoming shows and other activities. And they don't neglect the "old school" outlets like print or local broadcasting. A well-placed poster or radio spot can be attention-grabbing, and provide access to segments of the market that spend less time online (like many grandparents).

These strategies assure that when Cirque Maravilla is ready to arrive in a given area, the audience will be eagerly waiting. They can even purchase advance tickets and special VIP packages, which enhance their enjoyment of the event and make them feel more closely connected to the organization (plus make a little extra cash for the circus!). Remember that a savvy ringmaster is always on the look out for ways to provide the hors d'oeuvres and the limo ride as well as the steak.

Integrating your brand into the wider culture, especially the part of the culture occupied by your target markets is vital to your organization's health and survival. You must be vigilant and active, creating a reputation that is positive, and that is exactly what you intend it to be. Be aware of and intentional about your rep. Here's the real lesson of the Colorado plan: *Accentuate the positive and respond to the negative.*

When negatives arise — complaints, criticism, a logistical or financial setback, a public embarrassment, or a disaster — then you must deal with them quickly and affirmatively. Accept responsibility for any missteps.

Demonstrate that you are taking immediate and assertive action. Affirm your commitment to and affection for your client base and your employees. If you have done a good job building a brand that is appealing and respected, the public as well as your own staff is much more likely to be forgiving and encouraging if they have a firm belief in your heart and intentions.

8 - WHO LEFT THE CAGE OPEN?

The early fall days in his first year at the circus were some of the best years of Tino's young life. He quickly settled into a routine with the tiger crew, and Raj began letting him work directly with the oldest of the cats, Bara, who was calmer and less aggressive than the twins, Pasha and Parvati. Leila and Ruby had also given him more responsibility on the marketing team and so his salary had increased. His parents were relieved that his degree skills were being put to use after all and he felt like a pretty lucky guy.

By November, the weather had turned chilly. They were on the last leg of their tour, heading back towards New Jersey. The elephants had long since travelled back to their home in Florida and the acrobats needed a heater backstage. Even the tigers seemed a bit lethargic, hiding from the gusting winds in their shelters. The early sunset meant an earlier start for the show, so everyone had to hustle to be ready on time. One Friday afternoon, after lunch, Tino was jogging across the grass to meet a reporter who wanted to interview the clowns. He was hoping to be early so he could get a few minutes alone with

Jonelle, Leila's pretty new box office assistant. He rounded a corner, planning to sprint, and ran smack into Connor the juggler, knocking eight rubber balls in all directions. "Sorry, Clueless!" he yelped, brushing sawdust off his pants.

"Hey, watch the name-calling, Clumsy!" Connor shot back, but he smiled. "I'm only clueless about stuff that doesn't matter." He tossed Tino three of the balls, saying, "Show me how your basic skills are coming." Tino sighed, feeling the time slip away, but he paused to make a few moves. Connor had been really nice about showing him how, so he didn't want to be rude. After a moment, he tossed them back and apologized for needing to run off. Connor shrugged, "That's ok. I gotta find where the rest of those balls rolled." They parted ways.

He met the reporter right on time, gave her a quick tour of the grounds, and dropped her off at the clowns' trailer. Tino then circled back to the front of the property to make up for the lost time with Jonelle. After a promising fifteen-minute chat, he was on his way back to the tiger crew's area when Tino heard the dogs start barking frantically. This wasn't common, really as Sam and Eileen made sure of that. Some things did set them off occasionally such as a flock of birds or a stray cat but nothing big…until he heard the horses squealing in their pen. Something had spooked them big time and Tino broke into a run. He raced between concessions stands and around the tent to the back area where the animals were kept.

Weaving between crates he saw a flash of orange and white. "Oh no!" He thought. He knew that pattern. No one could mistake it. It was tiger skin. One of the cats was loose.

Tino got to the horses' pen to see Parvati a little ways in front of him. She had spied the horses, and was crouched low, stalking. Smelling the musky cat scent on the wind, they were beginning to panic. He moved forward quickly, wondering if he had time to run for back up before Parvati charged. Rita's crew poured from the trailer, and one of them rushed off immediately to find Raj and Dan. Rita herself stormed forward, riding crop in hand, ready to defend her animals, "How the hell did this happen, Tino?" She snapped over her shoulder.

"Keep your voice down, Rita," Tino replied, eyes on the cat. "You know Parvati won't like shouting. And there's a reporter in the clowns' trailer right now." In the background, the dogs yapped hysterically. He could see Eileen working to get them inside, but she was alone with ten frantic dogs of all sizes. It was going to take her some time to calm them, and he knew they'd have a crowd gathering soon.

"Oh just great," Rita growled, "Eddie, go get Leila. Fast and quiet. We got a potential PR nightmare here."

Tino grabbed a saddle blanket, hoping he could distract Parvati until the others arrived. He didn't have a chance to make his move, *though. One of the smaller dogs managed to leap the fencing around their enclosure, and came rushing forward. It launched itself straight at Parvati, latching on to her tail. It was enough to draw the cat's attention from the horses, which was a stroke of good luck for everyone. But it wasn't so lucky for the dog. Parvati lashed out with a giant paw, pinning the poor dog to the ground. The terrier let out one bite and one yelp of pain and then lay very still. Parvati sniffed it, growling. Then Raj, Dan, and the others strode into view. Tino could see they'd brought the emergency gear: the poles, a restraint, and the tranquilizer gun as a last resort. He moved forward to join them, and they went seamlessly into the procedure they'd practiced many times. They got quietly into place, and Dan called the cat. He coaxed her with a chunk of raw beef, tossed her a couple more, and patted her side. They drew her back towards the tiger enclosure with a game of 'catch the rag,' and as they approached Tino could see it was wide open. Fortunately, Bara and Pasha were sound asleep in their straw-lined beds.*

Raj sent Tino back to the horses' pen to get a situation update. He arrived to find Leila and one of the clowns telling the reporter a story about a camel that once got loose; she was doubled over with laughter. The little dog was nowhere in sight, and neither was Eileen. Rita's crew had moved the horses inside the tent; he could hear them talking in low, soothing tones. Ed Naeglin stood impassively to one side, arms crossed, and Tino joined him. "Does the reporter know?"

"Only that an animal got loose for a moment. She doesn't know which one. Everyone knows to stay cool, so she doesn't smell a crisis. And fortunately Johnny's great at suggestion; he won't lie about it, but she'll probably think it was a camel. I think the circus can avoid any bad PR. Eileen's going to be furious about her dog, though. And you can bet we'll be having a long meeting after the show tonight. All of us."

He returned to the tiger crew's trailer to find everyone sitting around a table. He gave them the update from Naeglin and Raj told him to sit down. It was one of the worst afternoons he had ever had. They went over and over the whole day—what everyone had done, where they had been—but they could not pinpoint how the enclosure door had been left unsecured. No one had gone in alone; everyone had confirmation from their partner that the latches had been properly locked down. No one could remember seeing a stranger or non-crew staff member anywhere near the enclosure. Finally, Raj stood with a sigh and left for Leila's office. Tino had the feeling that Raj was about to face the same grilling he had just given his crew.

The audience may not have known anything was amiss, but the staff was tense for the whole show. Eileen and Sam performed a modified act with half the usual dogs; some were still too upset to go on. Rita's horses were ok, but Raj kept Parvati out of the ring just to *be on the safe side. Naeglin was right. After the crowds had gone home, everyone gathered in the tent. There was no prelude. News travels fast in a traveling show and everyone knew what had gone down. Leila got right to the point, "Who left the cage open?" There was a long, uncomfortable silence. Then Connor stood up.*

"I think it must have been me. I took a spill kind of near the enclosure." He looked over at Tino, as if to say you remember, "And my stuff went everywhere. It took me forever to find the balls I had dropped. Turns out one of them rolled into the enclosure. It was right near the door, and the cats were all napping, so just I opened the door and got it. I thought I got the latch right, but I guess I didn't. I should have asked one of Raj's crew to get it for me, but I didn't want to bother them for something that would take 30 seconds." He sat back down and put his head in his hands. Leila spoke to everyone for about fifteen minutes more, reminding them of the importance of protocols and procedures, thanking them for keeping calm and keeping the reporter calm, too. Then she sent them off to bed.

The next morning Raj called another meeting. They sat around the table with coffee. No one looked like they had gotten much sleep, but he looked worst of all. "We had a bad day, yesterday," he started, "And we weren't the only ones. Leila feels strongly that we have to have zero tolerance where the tigers are concerned. So, Connor will be paying the cost to have Eileen's dog cremated, which is required by local laws. And he won't be finishing the season with us. She'll give him a good reference, but during the winter break we'll be hiring another juggling crew leader."

"Serves him right!" Dan complained, but Raj cut him short with a sharp tone.

"Did you see him open the enclosure, Dan? Did you stop him? Did I? Breakdowns don't happen in isolation. We made some mistakes yesterday, too, didn't we? As of today we're making some changes. For starters, the door is getting a padlock and no one gets in without a key. We're installing a camera, too. And any costs for a new dog—breeder's price, adoption fees, vaccinations, whatever—are coming out of our salaries. Now, why don't we start collectively brainstorming some other ways we might improve our procedures?"

Tino knew that things could have ended up a lot worse. Parvati could have attacked one of the horses or one of the staff. She could have wandered away from the circus grounds and been injured in traffic. The reporter could have taken a dim view of their safety practices and turned her lighthearted feature on circus clowns into a nasty exposé of Cirque Maravilla's animal treatment. But he still felt bad. He was sorry for Clueless Connor who was a nice guy and a good performer. He was sorry for Sam and Eileen, who loved their dogs like children.

He was also sorry for Leila and Raj, who had to make tough choices with consequences for everyone. He was especially sorry for his crew - he had never seen morale so low.

🖊 🖊 🖊 🖊

Every organization faces setbacks, obstacles, and even occasional disasters. Some of the bad things that happen are due to external factors beyond our control. Markets change. Tornados and fires occur. Governments change laws and regulations. In those situations, you do the best you can do respond with quick and innovative action.

But what do you do when the problem is caused by a person or persons inside your organization? Many a calamity has come from a mistake of commission or omission by someone who should have known better.

It's easy to play the "blame game" when something goes wrong, like Dan was tempted to do. While pinpointing the responsibility for a breakdown is an important part of the response, a leader's most important task is to fix the problem and prevent it happening again. As Raj demonstrated, that doesn't come from sitting around talking about how badly someone else screwed up. It is more important to diagnose the breakdown, come up with viable strategies to correct it, and act on them quickly.

Once a performance breakdown has been detected, the first step is to make any immediate changes needed to prevent the situation getting any worse. Get the tiger back in its enclosure ASAP. After that has been accomplished, it is necessary to take the steps that Leila took. Start by figuring out what caused it. The root cause of a breakdown can stem from a number of sources:

- People
- Processes
- Technology
- Administration/Policies
- Finances
- Product/Service
- Forces Majeure (otherwise known as "Acts of God") such as a hurricane, tornado or large, unforeseen events out of your control

What is the source of your problem? Did a person make a direct error? Are your processes incomplete, outdated, or flawed? Is your technology inadequate, obsolete, or broken? Are your administrative policies or procedures out of step or invalid? Are finances inadequate or mishandled? Is your product or service not meeting the market need, flawed, or outmoded?

Once you have pinpointed a source or sources, you must diagnose the nature of the breakdown.

- Was there a lapse in judgment?
- Has someone been subject to poor or inadequate training?
- Does one or more team member lack sufficient experience?
- Has there been a lack of supervision/management/oversight?
- Have personal issues or feelings been allowed to interfere in the work?
- Has there been a mismanagement or misuse of resources?
- Have equipment or facilities been allowed to become out of date or in disrepair?

While people, circumstances, and objects cannot be entirely controlled at any given moment, the leadership of any organization must monitor these things adequately and respond appropriately less a breakdown become a critical situation.

Your options for addressing breakdowns fall into two categories:

a) Whenever you can, you want to prevent breakdowns from occurring. Don't let the tiger escape its enclosure in the first place. Encourage mindful management. Have oversight procedures in place, carefully established routines, thorough review processes, cross-training and failsafe procedures ready to go. Establish clear lines of responsibility at every moment and articulate the consequences of failure. Have contingency plans in place. Provide feedback channels and a voice for all stakeholders; there should be accountability and performance critique for all levels.

Most of the time, the Cirque Maravilla runs like clockwork because Leila and all of the crew bosses pay close attention to these best practices. If they didn't, their patrons would suffer. Can you imagine: rats in the popcorn, falling acrobats, the human canon accidentally firing into the crowd? The circus itself would become a tiger on a rampage, and the local authorities would quickly put it out of everyone's misery.

b) When a breakdown does occur and it will, as all organizations are human organizations, you must respond appropriately to fix them. Act quickly. Engage in dynamic information-seeking and learn as much as you can about what went on. Talk to people; ask questions, and create an atmosphere where they can be truthful. Express compassion and empathy for those impacted, both inside and outside of your organization, and make a commitment to impact assessment. Analyze your alternatives using the best information available. Be self-reflective enough (as an individual leader and on the organizational level) to recognize if the problem is too large to be fixed from within. If you need it, get outside help from a consultant, mediator, or the like. And recognize that sometimes, like Leila, you must be willing to act decisively, even ruthlessly, to extract a 'lethal' cause.

When Parvati got loose, the collective response of the entire circus kept the incident from going critical. Sad as the fate of that poor terrier was, it could have been a lot worse than a single deceased canine. The fact that the members of each crew were well-prepared for how to handle an emergency, and that they all had a crystal clear understanding of the stakes and priorities, saved them from potential injury, financial loss, and public shame. They were even able to turn the reporter's presence into plus, without lying to her or engaging in any unethical behavior. Their confidence, competence, and calm gave her a positive view of the circus at a critical moment.

Leila and Raj displayed admirable leadership in the situation. While it was important that they uncover the source, neither of them made a public pariah of Clueless Connor. While Leila judged it best to let him go, she did so with compassion and assistance. Raj invited his team to help him assess the breakdown, and invited their input into the solution. He also laid out the consequences honestly and with authority, but avoided berating or abusing his team. Connor also did he try to shift the blame when it came to his own encounter with upper management.

A final word on breakdowns: There are few guarantees in business. Having breakdowns is one such guarantee, so it is best to anticipate them. In some organizations, there exist cultures of risk avoidance ("toe-the-line") that discourage the giving or receiving candid feedback. This leads to feedback gaps that may eventually lead to catastrophic events in the area of execution. Take, for instance, the NASA Challenger disaster where 7 astronauts were killed and the shuttle destroyed. Investigations discovered that NASA engineers knew there were critical flaws in the safety and cooling substructures. However, they did not bring it to the attention of their superiors because they feared for their jobs. NASA's work environment had been too caustic and mired in politics. Sadly, it took a significant loss of life and public investment to bring the organization's weaknesses to light.

If your tiger does get loose, be sure you are as prepared to handle the situation as the Cirque Maravilla.

9 - ETHICAL TIGER TAMING

Parvati's escape and Connor's departure cast a pall on the end of the season for everyone, although crowds were good to the last performance and the whole staff was looking forward to the holidays. Tino was ready to be off the road for a bit. There was a rumor that Jonelle might be joining them at the home office. He had some ideas about how a tiger tamer-in-training could market himself to a box office assistant.

A week into their spring strategy planning, Tino sat with Ruby in her office, researching the last season's tour routes for several competing shows. They were marking a map with colored flags when casually she said, "So, I notice you've got an appreciation for pink cornrow braids." He grinned, getting ready to tell her that he didn't need grandmotherly advice on girls or their funky hairstyles, but he noticed the look on Ruby's face. This was not going to be just a friendly chat. She was in full manager mode.

"Seriously, Tino. You've got to be careful about mixing work and romance. It happens a lot with traveling organizations, but we're still a business and we have policies. You do remember reading our guidebook on things like dating, our sexual harassment policies, and such? Or do I have to get out your signed copy?"

"Are you saying I can't take Jonelle out at all? Yeah, I remember reading those, and I didn't think it was prohibited if we weren't on the same crew."

"True. I won't tell you what to do. I'm just saying proceed with caution. Those policies were my idea, and they're a lot more comprehensive than most other shows in our biz. When I was young, I saw a lot of shenanigans go on and they're bad for business. Not to mention hard on people."

"I guess carnivals and circuses have kind of a seedy rap, don't they?" Tino replied. "Was it really that bad?"

"I was a receptionist at a big company for my first job. Then I worked with my uncle at a carnival until I met Leila's dad. I've seen plenty of cheating, dirty dealing, and bad behavior in both environments. It isn't just traveling shows that engage in shady business. The way I see it, companies can do a lot of good—creating jobs, prosperity for a town or even a country. But they have also done things that have ruined lives, wrecked economies, caused injury and death, even toppled governments." Ruby gestured to a photo of Leila's

father, Leonato "Leon" Maravilla on her desk. "What attracted me to Leila's dad was his integrity. He believed in treating his staff well, the animals better, and the rubes best of all. He didn't allow any of the typical P.T. Barnum bull to go on here."

"Ruby, your tiger tamer is from Jersey and you charge $10 for a souvenir book that costs $2 to make."

"That's showbiz, kid," Ruby shot back, laughing. "It's good business to create an entertaining spectacle and to charge what the market will bear for your product. But Leon used to drill everybody: we don't pull scams, we don't exploit or abuse anybody, and we try to make the communities we visit a happier place than we found them."

"Look," she went on, "We cover the obvious stuff like not dumping our animal waste illegally, actually serving 100% beef hotdogs because that's what sign says they are. But it's about more than just being honest. That's just where you start. It isn't easy to take the high road sometimes, especially when it cuts into your immediate profits. But we have found that it yields a lot of benefits. Choose your people wisely and treat them right, they'll stick around for years instead of taking off in the middle of the night like other shows. Do the maintenance on your bleachers and keep the audience safe, or you'll be dealing with lawsuits and fines. And why do you think Leila sends out those circus ambassadors to the hospitals and nursing homes? She's found a way to help people in need and create some good *press at the same time."*

Tino thought for a moment, "Yeah, I could see that on the road. I ate lunch with Rita's crew last week, and they were telling me that a lot of other circuses have trouble with the staff stealing from each other or the crowds. One of the things they like about Cirque Maravilla is that it doesn't happen here. In our public relations - those protesters in Colorado weren't ever going to change their minds about animal acts, but they couldn't complain about the way we treated them or how we handled their accusations. And I can think of a lot of places I've worked where nobody would have confessed to leaving the tigers' door open. If they did get caught, the managers at some of my old part-time jobs would have publicly strung them up. They wouldn't have been fair or polite about the whole thing, but Leila was...You know, I recognized all of that as ethical behavior, but I didn't think about that being something you have to intentionally create or cultivate."

"Tino, most of us are equally capable of good and bad behavior. You have to create an environment where everyone is more inclined to choose the former than the latter. Every organization has its own personality, and to a large degree, that is determined by the sum of the people who work for it. If it is run by people with no moral compass or ethical center, then it will have a negative impact on the world. They might make a bunch of money for a while, but when firms like Enron crash and burn they take a lot of people down with them. Fortunately,

it is also possible to run an organization that does well for itself and does good in the community. That's what Cirque Maravilla aims to be. That's the reputation we have, and it's the reason that towns and audiences trust us. It has gotten us through a lot of bad times, and it's why we expect to be around for a long while."

🐈 🐈 🐈 🐈

Every organization has the right to be concerned with its own survival. Especially for business, one of the goals is to stay in business. You gotta feed that tiger if you want to keep him alive, right? That's a perfectly acceptable philosophy, but it is equally important for leaders to be mindful about how you go about it. "Corporate responsibility" is a big buzzword right now, but it should be part of your company culture even when it stops being trendy to discuss it.

So how do you build an ethical organization, and why should it be a priority to do so?

First, let's consider what "ethical" ought to mean. Dr. A.R. Bernard, public speaker and founder of the Christian Cultural Center (a mega-church in Brooklyn with 11,000+ members), talks about the "Report Card for Adulthood."

He outlines three criteria for assessing individual behavior in the world: relationships, stewardship/management, and leadership. How well you perform at those three things is a sign of your character and maturity as a human being. I think the same three criteria could easily apply in judging the character of organizations. Ruby spelled it out for Tino: Organizations are as good, as trustworthy, and as praiseworthy as the leaders who steer them.

This doesn't mean you have to be a softie or a sucker. It doesn't mean being generous to a fault. Your organization will only survive if it is able to successfully do what it was built to do, whether that involves selling widgets or fundraising for the opera. What Leila has learned from her father Leon is that you can integrate making smart business decisions, drawing a crowd, and making a profit with corporate responsibility. The end goal is to leave your particular audience happier than you found them, and do it in a way that makes them want to reward you for doing it.

The three criteria on Bernard's report card cover several areas of ethical concern such as:

Relationships

1. How staff members are treated: Do they make a living wage and reasonable benefits? Are there opportunities for feedback and change? For advancement and improvement? Is there respect and cordiality in the work environment?

2. How clients/patrons/consumers are treated: Do they receive an appropriate level of service or product? Are there opportunities for feedback and change? Is their interaction with your organization pleasant and respectful?

3. How neighbors are treated: Does your presence create a disturbance? Are boundaries and property respected? Is any mess or pollution emitted? Do you clean up after yourselves?

4. How the public is treated: Do you contribute in some way to the community? Do you foster positive relations with local authorities? Do you representatives create a positive impression?

Stewardship/Management

1. How material resources are used: Do you attempt to conserve and use material resources wisely? Do you

take more than you need, or have a reputation for hoarding/using more than your fair share? Do you carefully account for materials, and maintain physical assets in good repair?

2. How time is spent: Do leaders and employees use time wisely? Is the organization focused on executing on its mission, or is it easily distracted?

3. How the physical environment is managed: Does the organization generate waste or byproducts? How are those handled? Is workplace safety a priority? Environmental conservation? Are buildings, machines, etc., clean and in good repair? Does the organization manage and minimize its impact on the local environment/landscape?

Leadership

1. How profit is perceived and pursued: Are your guidelines for pursuing profit carefully outlined? Are all local and national laws/regulations followed with regard to making money and paying taxes? Is there a perception that profit motive outranks all other human or social considerations? Are dishonest or

"gray" practices tolerated or encouraged within the company?

2. How values are respected and reflected: Do all organizational members understand and commit to upholding company core values? Are those core values clearly articulated, and do they harmonize with ethical and social norms for the community? Are the personal values of organizational members understood and respected?

3. How the community is affected: Does the organization articulate an understanding of its footprint in the community? Does it articulate understanding and empathy for the community's needs and expectations? Are there programs in place to contribute positively to the life of the community?

Your relationships, stewardship, and leadership always drive the overall perception of your business. But what will matter most is what you do when things are hard. When there is plenty of business, plenty of money, and plenty of opportunity, most people find making ethical choices a lot easier. Even if you don't go around being a do-gooder, at least it isn't nearly so tempting to do harm—either by conscious action or by neglect. Downturns happen though. Natural disasters happen too. Accidents happen also. Tigers get loose.

When hard times hit your organization, leadership must always face some hard choices. Sometimes layoffs and other cutbacks are necessary. You may have to let go of someone who is popular or who has tried hard. You might have to apologize and make amends for an error that has harmed one or more people. There could be fines to pay, property to replace, or lives lost. What people will remember is how your leadership behaves during such periods. This is equally true for your customers, your employees, and the general public. Those are the times that you and your colleagues will be getting those Report Cards for Adulthood. It is important to remember as you make choices, when things are going well or when disaster strikes, that you will be judged on the quality of your relationships, stewardship, and leadership as much as any specific outcome.

10 - TAKING A BREATHER

As he started his third year with Cirque Maravilla, Tino felt that he had settled into a good routine. He understood the organization's rhythms, and its structure. He knew many of the people well, and felt that some of them were now his friends as well as his co-workers. Thanks to Ruby's stories about dysfunctional shows, he understood and valued the spirit of cooperation that prevailed here. His folks were still a little discomfited by how much time he spent on the road, but were proud that he was growing his marketing skills. He now felt like a real member of his crew, even if Dan was still a jerk. Raj had also given him some one-on-one training with the cats during the season break, showing him how to read their body language and direct their behavior in the ring. As a result, he got a little stage time in the act this season. He was able to trade his grey jumpsuit for red and black, like Dan and Francine wore. Sometimes as he drifted off to sleep in *his bunk, he couldn't believe this was actually his life. He'd run away and joined the circus for real, and so far it was working out just fine.*

The first three months of the season went by in a blur as the circus travelled down the East Coast and then swung toward the Deep South. Everything had ticked along so smoothly that no one on the tiger crew was prepared for Raj's bombshell news. The morning they pulled into Tulsa, after the enclosures were set up and the tigers were absorbed in their breakfast, Raj sat them down for a crew meeting. They went over the day's responsibilities—the normal stuff—and then he announced, "In August I'll be taking a break. So you all need to start thinking now about how you'll pick up the slack."

"A break?"

"How long will you be gone?"

"Wait, you're going somewhere?"

Everyone was talking at once. Raj held up a hand to signal for quiet. "I need to take a breather," he said. "I haven't had any real time off in over seven years, and I'm feeling run down. Plus, I'd like to get current on some information on big cats. I don't get a lot of free time around here, and that's going to take some concentration and in-depth study. So first I'm going to India to see family and spend time at a meditation center. In the fall, I'll be taking a couple of classes at the university near the home office. I'll be back on the job in January to help plan the season, and then resume touring next spring."

"*Does Leila know you're going?*" Tino blurted out, and then immediately thought, *Aah. I sounded like a fourth grader.* Dan shot him a look of contempt, but Raj just laughed.

"*I wouldn't be telling all of you if I hadn't cleared it with her first. She agrees that I'm due for a break and some continuing ed. I wanted to tell all of you now, so you'll have plenty of time to prepare yourselves for the added responsibilities. I'll be talking to each of you individually this afternoon, and tomorrow we'll go over the breakdown.*"

Tino was stunned. He had to focus hard to give his chores the attention they needed. And when it was his turn to sit with Raj alone, he had to restrain himself from saying something stupid like *I can't believe you're ditching us!* He knew Raj deserved a break as much as anyone, and more than most. The tamer worked really hard. It was just that he still felt he had a lot to learn from Raj, and would miss the advice and attention he had been receiving. He listened quietly while Raj conducted what was basically a performance review of his recent progress, and nodded seriously as his mentor talked him through some strategies for coping with potential personality conflicts. Raj hadn't named names, but he knew the message was, "*Don't get into it with Dan while I'm gone.*" He was at least gratified that Raj was giving him responsibility for maintaining the brand management in his absence. "*You'll have some extra weight to carry in addition to your usual job, just like the others. Can I count on you to keep up?"*

Tino was a little nervous, but didn't hesitate and said, "YES."

Later that night, as he was brushing his teeth, a new thought struck Tino. Raj was going away. Raj was dividing his responsibilities among the crew. So who was going to take his place in the ring? He thought back to Dan's expression at their meeting that morning and he knew that Dan was already thinking about the same thing.

He didn't have to wait long to find out. At the next morning meeting, Raj declared, "Ok, we've got it worked out. Hiro will coordinate directly with Sergei on the tigers' health and feeding. Josh and Jamie, you'll be the ones to communicate with Naeglin about our equipment. Francine will handle any ordering or communications with the office, and will back up Tino on our branding and marketing. Dan has the most experience, so he will coordinate everyone and monitor the tigers. He's team leader until I return."

"That just leaves one more thing. Someone will have to step into my role in the show. I think its best for the cats if we use one person instead of creating a rotation for the spotlight. So if you're interested, talk to me this afternoon. We will have auditions in a few weeks."

From the looks on their faces, it was clear that neither Tino nor Dan could quite believe their ears. But if Dan had expected to have the job handed to him, he quickly covered, adopting a more neutral expression. Tino's face lit with hope. H e had pretty much assumed that it was a done deal. But if he really had a chance, he better start preparing now.

🐾 🐾 🐾 🐾

Raj's plans for a sabbatical might have come as a surprise to his team at first, but as a leader, he understands the need to nurture his own growth and well-being even as he monitors the progress of his team and the happiness of his tigers. Believe me, there is nothing New Age or "touchy-feely" about this. Why does it matter? Shouldn't the people in charge be able to muscle through any difficulties without burdening others? Absolutely not! No one is suggesting that it is acceptable for the boss to be a whiner, but you need to recognize that, as a human being, your body, mind, and spirit require the same attention and proper maintenance as any of your other valuable resources. Sometimes being a good leader involves a realization that your own life is out of balance, and taking action before it affects the quality of your work and has a negative impact for your whole organization.

Taking a break is not just about self-discovery...though living according to the "adult report card" is hard work. Taking time for refreshment/recharging will keep you from the burnout that causes leaders to let everything from their attention to their ethics slide. It can also be about renewing/updating your own competencies and skills. When you lead others, sometimes you let your own growth fall by the wayside. No leader wants to be out of date or irrelevant, so pay attention to yourself along with your team.

Good leaders are those who are able to sustain their success over the long term. They understand that their own happiness and health affects what they bring to the table at the organizations they serve. As much as you can say you leave your interior feelings or your personal life at the door of the office, no one really does. So it matters to keep yourself healthy, happy, and growing. An important key to doing that is integrating your work life into your whole life.

What does it mean to have work and life balance? When the major areas of responsibility in your life are well integrated, you will notice the following:

1. Work is enjoyable.
2. Your personal life is enjoyable.
3. You are effective.
4. You are aware and alert.

5. You sense that you are "on."

6. Others have confidence in your competence.

7. Your decisions and actions yield good fruit.

Of course, this does not mean that every day will be filled with bliss and delight. There will still be challenges to meet and vexations to overcome. But you will find satisfaction in doing your work. If you have a bad day, you will comfort yourself that good days are also coming. You will not be plagued with the feeling that things will never get better.

If you find that one or more of these six elements are not in alignment, then it may be time for you to take a breather. If your recent assessments from supervisors and colleagues are not positive, if you are noticing pushback or dissatisfaction from coworkers/family/friends, or if you are just feeling run down and out of step, then you may be out of balance and integration. You need to make some changes or you are going to end up tiger food. It is time to pull back, make assessments, and maybe reset.

Once you have diagnosed the problem ("My life is out of balance"), the next step is to decide what remedy is in order in your case. This can be tough. In fact, it is where many ambitions for change break down. Figuring out the right course is so confusing, so daunting, that many people decide just to ignore the problem and hope it will sort itself out. But it rarely does. If you have determined that you are in a rut or on course for a breakdown, ask yourself the following:

- What does the proper remedy look like for me?
- Does it mean changing something in the work or personal environment?
- Does it mean shedding or adding some responsibilities?
- Does it mean getting new training or education?
- Does it mean a brief vacation or retreat?
- Does it mean walking away completely for a time ("leaving the world")?

Discerning this requires reflection. Give yourself the time. Take an afternoon off work or ask your spouse to take the kids while you journal over coffee for a couple of hours. Don't be afraid to share your thoughts with someone, especially if your situation is going to have an impact on others. Go to a supervisor or mentor, a respected peer or personal advisor (friends, family, priest, etc.). Take care that anyone you choose to share with is: a) a person you respect, b) someone who shows evidence of having a balanced life of their own, and c) has an investment in your personal and professional success.

Once you have a solid idea of what your remedy looks like, you need to take action to make it happen. A treatment plan is great, but if you don't follow the doctor's advice and take the medicine, do you get better? Of course not! Here are the steps you need to take:

1. Come up with a specific plan. Know what it is you want to do. Know what the impact of your absence will be as well as the ultimate benefit of the breather. It is a good idea to do any research needed and write everything down.

2. Get buy in from personal and organizational stakeholders. Remember: first Raj cleared his sabbatical with his boss, Leila. Then he sat his team down and explained to them why it was needed and how they would meet the challenge of his absence. He also met with each of them individually to make sure they were

all committed and aligned.

3. Secure financial and logistical means to make it happen. Whether it is a vacation, a workshop, a training, a job move, or any other change, you need to be prepared for the financial burdens and the potential upheaval it may cause for you and for others. If you have a good plan and can demonstrate the positive impact for your organization, it is perfectly appropriate to ask for their help and support. But if outside resources are not available to achieve your goal, have a Plan B in place for how you can accomplish it on your own.

4. Commit 100% to being present for whatever your breather is.

The best organizations make this part of their culture. Consider the technology consulting and management company, Accenture. Not only do they provide resources to help their employees stay educated about important topics for both their work and personal lives (everything from health to legal advice), they provide a sabbatical program featuring one month unpaid leaves of absence.

Any employee may request a sabbatical once every three years. The company will consider any proposal that will improve the employee's work or personal life, and will help them develop a savings plan to reserve part of of their salary for the purpose. Many employees consider it one of the best benefits of working for the company.

Your organization may have the will and the resources to make taking a breather part of its culture. But like Raj, you need to pay attention to the signs in your own life and know when you are due for a change. Take the initiative and come up with one or more plans that will make it easy for your ringmaster to say "yes" and anticipate the return of the refreshed, improved you.

11 - ARE YOU TIGER FOOD?

Three weeks. That was how much time Tino had to get ready. The auditions would take place right after the July 4ᵗʰ show, when the whole circus took a two-day rest. Raj wanted the rest of the month to work privately with his chosen replacement and prepare that person to assume the starring role in the act. He had never attacked a project with this level of desire or intensity.

In the moments after Raj's announcement that the spotlight was up for grabs, Tino had thought "Heck yeah, I'm going for it!" Later that night, when Jamie and Josh were snoring the way only contented men can, he began to have doubts. He thought back to the tiger cologne incident, and how his ignorance had put Sergei and Raj in danger, not to mention the embarrassment that followed. He thought about Clueless Connor, and wondered if he couldn't have done more to help the juggler avoid the near-disaster that followed their accident. He recalled the conversations on showmanship and branding that he and Raj had shared, and thought about how much the tiger act meant to the circus and its ability to draw crowds and stay profitable. Was he really ready to step into Raj's boots? In the ring, the act succeeded or failed on the skills of the tamer and the lives of the crew could be in the balance, too! If he made a big mistake, someone could end up tiger food. Maybe him!

When he got up the next morning, Tino decided however that he owed it to himself to at least try. He had learned a lot in the last two years, and he wanted to get to the next level. He might not win the prize this time, but the experience of reaching for it could be worthwhile on its own. If he failed utterly, he'd at least know it might be time to consider a different profession - maybe tightrope walking? He knew the first thing he needed was some honest self-reflection, which would help him decide how to proceed. During his lunch break the next day, Tino retired to the quiet of the trailer and made a list. He created two columns on the same piece of paper with the left column titled "Why I should try out" and the right, "Why I should wait."

Why I Should Try Out	*Why I Should Wait*
1. It is why I joined the circus.	1. I have only been doing this for 2 years.
2. I have worked hard.	
3. I want to help the circus succeed.	2. I have made some mistakes that could have had serious consequences.
4. I understand the circus's mission.	
5. I am a good performer.	3. Others have more experience.
6. I can add some fresh ideas.	4. I haven't had the spotlight at Cirque Maravilla yet.
7. The audience will like me better than Dan.	5. Raj has suggested several areas for improvement. I need to work on those.
8. I know a lot about tigers.	
9. Raj has taught me some great techniques.	6. The other crewmembers might not be ready to support me.
10. The tigers like me.	
11. Raj has faith in me.	7. Tigers are wild animals. They can be unpredictable.
12. My performance reviews have been positive.	8. The stakes for failure are very high.
	9. Leila might not think I'm ready.
	10. This is bigger than anything I have done.

Tino went over his recent reviews. He considered how the extra responsibility would impact his current work. Tino still felt it would be worthwhile to audition, so it seemed like the next step would be to ask for an outside opinion. He decided to talk to Josh and Jamie first. If his peers thought he was crazy, he probably shouldn't ask the boss. That evening, he asked what they thought of the idea.

"It's not that crazy, man," shrugged Jamie, "You've done a lot with what Raj taught you during the break."

"Dan's got a lot more years of experience, but you're a good showman," suggested Josh. "Give it a shot."

So the next day, Tino went to Raj and asked his approval to try. "It's a little soon, Tino," said his boss thoughtfully, "But the preparation might be a learning opportunity. I think we should run it by Leila, since you are important to the marketing team. You can't let your regular work slide."

Tino understood, and when he saw Leila that afternoon, he was ready. He explained why he wanted the chance to audition, laid out his plans for making sure his current work got done, and a preparation plan for his audition that made use of his free time. In the end, his name added to the pool of applicants.

For the next three weeks, he was a madman. He scrubbed tiger cages, chopped tiger chow, wrote tiger copy for press releases, and read *tiger books. He watched the footage Raj provided them of famous big cat tamers, spent time in the enclosure under Dan's watchful eye, and asked other performers for suggestions and feedback. The day of the audition, he felt ready. This has been more work than any internship or scholarship interview I've ever done, he thought. Each of the three applicants - Dan, Francine, and Tino - had fifteen minutes to take the tigers through a routine with Josh, Jamie and Hiro for support. The heads of each performing crew stood in for the audience.*

Dan's routine was technically perfect. The tigers knew him well, and did exactly as he asked when he gave the signal. He could get them to do some impressive tricks that Tino knew better than to try, like balancing on the giant rubber ball. But he didn't have much personality in the ring. He was concentrating hard and forgot to smile, even scowled once or twice. He seemed to forget that the audience needed to connect to him, too. So, when it was his turn, Tino felt confident. He was less commanding than Dan, true, and he stuck to the basic moves he knew best. But he integrated some of what he'd learned from his time with other crews: juggling bits of tiger meat, adding flourishes that Sam and Eileen preferred, tossing each cat a flower the way Rita sometimes did her horses. He made one misstep: moving too swiftly in a way that made Pasha raise a paw and swipe at his side. The cat was only annoyed and not angry. Pasha intended only to warn him, but Tino knew it would count against him. Both guys had done well, he knew. But in the end, it was Francine who really took over the stage. She stepped into the ring with sparkle and personality. She treated the cats with both authority and affection, and took them through the moves in a way that kept the pace quick and exciting. Raj and Leila's choice was clear, and it surprised no one when the announcement was made the next day that Francine would take Raj's place.

Tino was still glad he had tried. He had learned a lot and was proud of his own effort. Raj complimented his style and inventive performance; Leila allowed that given a few years, he might have the makings of a star. The praise felt good. Most surprising, and perhaps even more gratifying, was the conversation with Dan that night. After the show, he sat on the steps of his trailer sipping a beer. The others had gone out to celebrate a trapeze artist's birthday. Dan appeared out of the dark, took a bottle from the cooler, and sat next to him. "Francine's a sneaky one, isn't she? Who knew there was a competitor under that quiet exterior?" He said.

Tino laughed and nodded. "I figured you'd get the gig. You've got the most experience, so you had the edge."

"Yeah, so did I," Dan admitted, rubbing his jaw. "I can admit that she earned it, and I didn't. I haven't given enough thought to the audience connection side of this, and I see now how much that matters. I just love big cats; all I ever think about is them. And Raj does it all

so well, makes it look so natural, that I never thought about it. But I looked at the video from my audition, and I'm completely stiff. Your performance looked great, though. You made everybody laugh, you made them like you instantly."

"But you never would have made that mistake with Pasha," Tino countered.

"I tell you what," Dan said, "Raj will be busy with Francine's private coaching until August. Then we're both going to be backing her up for a few months. Maybe we can help each other. I'll help you read the cats' body language a little better. You can give me some ideas on bringing a little more flare to my presence in the ring."

Would wonders never cease? Tino thought to himself, amazed and humbled. "That sounds great," Tino replied. He said nothing else, wanting this moment to last. Instead, the two tamers in training sat quietly, sharing a beer and staring at the stars.

🐾 🐾 🐾 🐾

Tino may not have won the prize, but the path he took to auditioning demonstrates how much he has grown in his years with the Cirque Maravilla. It is true that reaching for the things you want takes courage and involves risk, and you must be prepared for that. Just make sure the risks you take are carefully considered. Tino's actions in this situation amounted to more than reaching for his dream promotion. He created an opportunity to demonstrate his growing knowledge and maturity to the major influencers and decision makers of his organization. This was the result of careful self-assessment. Tino is now one step closer to achieving his dream. If he had taken a less cautious approach, neglected to get buy-in from the major stakeholders, or failed to take careful stock of his current skills, he might have destroyed that dream entirely.

Self-assessment is more than just deciding whether you are happy or in need of a break. It is about constant awareness of your skill levels, your current performance, your place in the organization, and your opportunities and potential over the long term. If you do not self-assess continually and well, the risks are greater than losing the audience's applause. You might get eaten!

Self-assessment is a process with multiple steps that will need your careful attention. But if you learn and follow them religiously, it should give you a very clear picture of your current situation. This can be especially helpful if you are struggling, fearful of losing your place, or like Tino, you want to advance in your career. Keep in mind the following steps:

- Review the established performance standards for your organization. Learn them inside and out.
- Review your feedback and evaluation from others. Get clarity on where you stand in relation to those standards.
- Notice who the high performers are in your organization. Observe what they do well. Compare yourself to them. (Be honest, but don't be too harsh.)
- Assess what it takes for you to become a high performer yourself. What must you do? What must you commit? Be honest about your ability/willingness to do so.
- Do these things in a consistent, timely fashion.

At the end of your reflection, your conclusions will either be positive or negative. Either you will feel confident that you are on the right track, or you will realize that you are in a downward spiral. While it is important to trust your gut, remember that sometimes your gut lies so you need facts - fast. Whether you are confident in your situation or not, recognize that you have room to improve.

If your assessment is positive, you can begin thinking about taking a place in the center ring. Like Tino, you will need to do the following:

- Develop a personal development plan and some goals
- Get more feedback from others
- Get a mentor to help you grow and progress
- Actively pursue development opportunities
- Determine the best course for advancement (within your current organization or elsewhere)
- Execute on growth/advancement opportunities. Go for it!

If your assessment is negative, you could be at risk of being devoured or getting someone else eaten. If your gut is saying the boss is about to cut you loose, don't ignore it. This can start with a bad evaluation, or emerge from self-reflection (this is preferable to the former). In this case, take the following steps:

- Take feedback to heart and commit to making changes
- Re-organize your work approach. Use tangible 30, 60, 90 goals
- If you need additional training or education and take steps to get it
- Decide if you need mentoring or personal attention and ask for it
- Honestly consider whether this role is a good fit for you—especially if the first four steps are not helping. If they are not, it may be time to walk away
- If you decide to fold and walk, do so with dignity. Don't burn bridges
- Take steps to determine what's next. Don't leap without looking. It's ok not to have a perfect plan in place sometimes, but do what you can.

You should monitor the life of your organization as closely as you do your own situation. Maybe the writing is on the wall for your business. There can be external forces in play that can have an impact. Maybe the economy is down, or maybe they are making other changes. You need to have situational awareness in these cases. Self-assessment will also help you to deal with the repercussions of those external forces that you cannot control. They can help you decide when to get out, how to anticipate change, and what to do if you think a job loss is immanent.

Emerging professionals like Tino are not the only ones who live or die by self-assessment. Plenty of high profile careers have been ended by a lack of situational awareness (remember Connor the Juggler?). In 2005, the sports world witnessed a painful effort to revitalize the Ladies' Professional Golf Association by Carolyn Bivens. As commissioner, she had a powerful vision on how to bring the organization into the new millennium and revive its fortunes. Unfortunately, she communicated badly with key stakeholders. A number of long-time sponsors fell away and the primary new sponsor was crippled by the 2008 financial crisis. She signed important new deals for broadcasting and increasing player fees, but instituted a series of unpopular regulations that angered many players. In the end, she resigned before her plans could come to fruition. In essence, she was a leader with many good ideas and drive, but did not foresee the negative impact of her management style. Had she engaged in more careful self-reflection and taken feedback from her peers, many of the worst problems could have been avoided.

Tino, on the other hand, is enjoying what could be called a "successful failure." He has new knowledge that he can now apply to his daily efforts; his reflection and preparation have given him experience that will serve him well now and in future audition; moreover, his supervisors and peers have increased respect for him, having seen how he was able to temper his ambition with hard work and openness to feedback. Tino has successfully transitioned from would-be tamer to tamer-in-training, with the very real prospect of tamer-in-chief bright on his horizon.

12 - ASSESSING YOUR SHOW

November in Ohio, thought Tino, hustling across the grounds toward the tiger enclosure on a particularly brisk and frosty morning. He wondered if one of the tigers would mind if he crawled in their straw-lined bed. I might get shred-ded, but at least I'd be warm. His responsibilities made him get up earlier these days, which meant lots of walking around the camp in the cold. Tino would have to invest in a better jacket during the winter break. Maybe Josh or Jamie would lend him an extra fleece for today. The big end-of-season crew head meeting was this afternoon, and he expected to be running back and forth across the grounds on errands for Leila.

As he stepped into the trailer, he was already calling, "Hey guys, do you have a" but the room was empty. He checked the office trailer next door where coffee was made every morning. That was empty too. Where was everyone? It was early for them to be up and away from home base. The tigers didn't stir before 9 am when it was too hot or cold. But he thought he'd check their en-closure anyway.

Tino found the whole crew inside the enclosure, looking extremely worried. Sergei was in the enclosure, too, kneeling near one of the bed crates. Francine and Dan were close behind him, and the three were talking in low voices. "What's wrong?" he asked, stepping in next to Hiro. Hiro replied, "Bara's sick. We're not sure what's wrong but she can't get up and I think she's in pain."

This was worse than bad news. They all cared for the cats. Losing a part of their most popular act could have serious revenue consequences. Tino couldn't bear the idea of the big cat show disappearing. He was filled with dread. Tino watched Francine step away from the crate and dial her cell phone. She paced back and forth as she talked for about five minutes, and then shoved the phone back in her pocket. Sergei and Dan stood up. They conferred for a couple of tense moments and Sergei pulled out his own phone. Then Dan called out, "Josh, Jamie, Hiro. Help me move Parvati and Pasha into the practice ring. They won't want to leave their crates, so get the special treats out. Tino, you're with Francine." The little group broke up as they hurried to help. As Tino approached, he could see Bara in her bed. She was panting hard, her head and shoulders straining. Her front paws were twitching, but her back legs wouldn't seem to move. Sergei hung up and turned to face them, "I've got a truck coming and some of Naeglin's stronger guys. We'll load her in the back. Leila's contacted the local zoo and they gave us the name of an animal hospital that should have the equipment I need. If we can avoid surgery I might be able to make it back for the meeting. Otherwise I'll have to talk to Leila about it."

"Dan will ride with you," Francine replied, "We both know no one can talk him out of coming along! I'll have Joey bring me in about an hour. I've got to make arrangements for this afternoon. I should stay with Bara and try to reach Raj." She turned to Tino. "I was supposed to sub for Raj at the meeting, but that's a no-go now. I've already talked to Leila about it, and she agrees that you should sit in for the tiger crew. Come sit with me in the office and I'll go over everything with you before I go." Seeing Tino's expression, she laughed a little. "Don't worry. If you handle everything the way I say, you'll be fine."

Tino was excited and nervous simultaneously. I finally can be part of the tiger crew, he thought. At last! He was elated but also wary.

Later that day, Tino joined Leila in the main tent. The head of each crew was already seated around a large makeshift table inside the tent. The ringmaster wasted no time. As soon as everyone was seated, she called the meeting to order. "Thanks for being on time, everyone. Of course, Cirque Maravilla doesn't hire anyone without a sense of *timing, so I expect no less. I know is on everyone's mind, so I'll start with an update our sick tiger. Bara is at a local veterinary hospital."*

Nodding to the animal doctor who had just walked in, she went on, "According to Sergei, her ailment is not a digestive disease or a new injury. It is most likely arthritis, which happens to a lot of performers as they get to a certain age." Some of the performers, especially the acrobat and trapeze boss, laughed a bit.

"She has some inflammation that makes it too painful to walk. So we'll get her on medication and take her out of the ring. Raj will decide where we go from there. That's all any of us can do about it right now, so let's get down to business," and then there was a general murmuring and shuffling of paper as they prepared to get to work.

Tino had expected to be at the meeting because Leila often wanted his help. However, he found that sitting in Raj's chair made it a different experience. First, they went over team assessments. This was familiar to Tino, since he had spent so much time considering performance reviews for his recent audition. But he paid close attention to how the crew heads talked about their team and noted which ones were diplomatic, which ones complained directly about specific people, and whether each one was careful and reflective about how their crew fit into the bigger picture. Tino also watched Leila offer feed-back. She added in employee comments from recent management surveys in a way that gave each crew boss clear direction without bruising any egos.

He read Raj's report, silently noting how it accurately addressed their current strengths and weaknesses without singling anyone out for criticism. He went over the printed list of Raj's requests for equipment and training tools, and shared the team's plan for continued training and professional development in the coming year. As Francine advised him earlier, Tino was careful to speak plainly and to choose his words wisely. He made it clear that the ideas and assessments were Raj's, and that he understood his role as a messenger clearly. "Remember," Francine told Tino, "Most of them like you, and they value what you've helped the marketing team achieve. But you are still young, and most of them have been been circus folk for 15 or more years. If you seem too eager or pompous, they won't like it at all." So Tino took pains to be as respectful as possible. When he finished, and Ed Naeglin clapped him roughly on the back and said, "Good job, kid," Tino felt like he'd won the lottery.

Each team was asked to put forward the names of their "top performer" for the year. The whole group (excluding Tino and a couple of other junior staffers) then voted on the two most deserving of the "Maravilla Center Ring" award, which came with a generous annual bonus. Leila also announced the amount of the smaller bonuses that would be available for each crew boss if they wanted to recognize one or more team members in a more localized way. She reminded them that the criteria included showing marked improvement in skills, consistent *performance, and going above and beyond in their expected job parameters. Finally, a new award, the "Circus Hero," would be implemented starting the following season. These would be awarded once a quarter, and would recognize anyone who had done something remarkable: a unique act of kindness, bravery in the face of danger, or genuine excellence in customer service. The reward would include a gift certificate to a store chosen by the crew boss, a special meal in the canteen, and recognition in the circus newsletter. Ti-no noted with approval that most of the crew heads really enjoyed this part of the meeting, and seemed eager to recognize strong performance by individual employees.*

Sergei and the circus physician, "Doc," both had opportunities to report on the health and wellbeing of both animals and staff. They both praised crews where safety, nutrition, and good protocols were followed. Doc also warned about some injury risks he had observed among the clowns and acrobats, urging their crew bosses to be more vigilant. Tino had never really thought about the effects of accidents or ill health on the circus as a business. He realized how important both Sergei and the Doc were for the long-term success of the organization.

Next, Leila offered her assessment of the company as a whole. She worked in the information received from the crew heads' reports, laid out her expectations for how each team would operate over the next tour season, and indicated any areas where improvement was needed. Tino admired how she laid things out in a matter-of-fact way, offering a mix of praise and criticism without embarrassing anyone, and phrased her expectations clearly and concisely.

Finally, Ruby who flew in just for this meeting every year even though airplanes terrified her, stood to give the strategic report. She reminded every-one of the goals from the current year, using a PowerPoint presentation to show charts and reports that tracked their progress. She went over the circus's current product offering, which included their show receipts, the collateral merchandise, and concessions. She asked the crew heads to brainstorm new ideas for expanding their portfolio, and set a deadline for their responses. Ru-by also reminded everyone of the key performance indicators (KPI) they used to assess the organization's health such as profitability, customer ratings and reviews, animal and staff well-being, employee satisfaction, and environmental impact. Then Leila outlined places were improvement was possible such as greater waste reduction; updating some of the acts; composing new music; and monitoring workloads for crews with high levels of exhaustion. Last, they celebrated the circus's great critical and audience reviews in the traditional press and social media. There was no show that night and a special meal awaited everyone in the canteen. They adjourned the meeting in high spirits.

Tino stayed behind to clear away the papers and stack the chairs. He looked forward to sitting with Jonelle at dinner and telling her what he'd learned - at least, as much as he could share. As he reflected on the discussion, he thought about a well-known leadership book that he read his junior year in college, Good to Great by Jim Collins. In particular, he remembered what Collins said about the best leaders, who "embody a paradoxical mix of personal humility and professional will. They are ambitious, to be sure, but ambitious first and foremost for the company, not themselves." Tino realized that he'd seen for himself what Collins meant.

✦ ✦ ✦ ✦

A thorough annual review process is essential for the health of any organization. Most employees won't think beyond their own immediate performance assessment; Tino didn't give it much mental energy himself until he saw the process in action. Now he under-stands that leaders have to consider operational strengths and weaknesses at all levels: their own individual contribution, the work of their team, the coordination between teams, and high-level activity.

The information garnered from assessments should be integrated at all levels. It starts with each employee's self-assessment and his or her performance reviews from management. These two assessments help each individual understand his or her role in the bigger picture of the company's goals. It is similar to Tino, Dan, and Francine answering the question, "Am I tiger food or am I a star?" Managerial assessments and team assessments should be done to evaluate how the different parts of the machine work together, and whether fi-ne tuning, adjustment, or new parts may be needed. While most companies cannot operate as democracies, it is important that the feedback chain operate in both directions.

Top-grading, recognition, and reward policies also provide a number of benefits. Every year, Tino has witnessed how eagerly the circus staff awaits the announcement of the Center Ring awards and the bonuses. He knows these announcements have a profound impact on motivation and morale. The back-stage crew and support staff seem especially appreciative, since they never get to enjoy the roar of the crowd. People work harder when they have an expectation of something desirable, whether it is money or applause. Thanks his participation in the annual meeting, he now sees that the opportunity to recognize and reward staff can have value to upper management, as well. They appreciate the positive effect it can have when well-managed and relish the opportunity to celebrate employee success.

Strategic planning also depends on full coordination inside the organization. The Cirque Maravilla could never successfully execute on their yearly goals if they did not get the entire company aligned and all the circus members pulling in the same direction.

Rita might wish that she could focus on nothing else but riding horses all day, but she knows that there will be no center ring if the crowds don't come with their pocketbooks open. So she makes sure her whole crew knows exactly what the product offering is, how they contribute to it and what their areas of responsibility are. Leila also makes it clear that if any given department slacks off, she will figure out why using key performance indicators (KPI) that will reveal where the breakdown is. Everyone knows that she will not hesitate to take remedial action if necessary, including cutting chronic under-performers. Leila expects that every crew member follows the same policies throughout the company consistently.

As the Cirque Maravilla makes its way back toward New Jersey for the winter break, the staff will be focused on the things that they know will help the organization meet its goals for the year. The crew bosses know they are responsible for providing creative and practical ideas that Ruby and her team can use as they plan for the new season. They are also confident that their suggestions, requests, and advice will be given serious and thoughtful consideration. Many of them will see their best ideas implemented by the spring.

Sometimes, Tino still doubts whether some of those bosses share Leila's appreciation for the big picture. He knows that most of them are happiest when they are concentrating on their own small sphere of influence, with the team that they know and appreciate best. But having spent the afternoon observing them under the right circumstances, he also knows that they see the circus as a kind of living thing and that it requires as much care and attention as Bara, Parvati, Pasha, the horses, or any other individual part of the whole. He also knows that the projects that began in the home office will be seen through to completion by people who are very good at what they do.

CONCLUSION – THE SHOW MUST GO ON

Leila and Tino sat on either side of her desk in the little office trailer, waiting for Raj. It was April and the weather was fine outside. He could hear the different acts rehearsing, and the dogs yapping cheerfully in the distance. Everyone was always in a good mood during the spring leg of the tour. Tino was hunched over a laptop, updating social media profiles, when the tiger tamer walked in. Raj was looking like his sabbatical had done him a world of good. Sometimes Tino felt guilty that he had not noticed how tired Raj had been in the last six months before his break.

Raj laughed, clapping Tino's shoulder in a friendly way, and said, "Just think, Leila. It was about three years ago that Tino stood in that doorway, trying to talk us into letting him walk right into that tiger cage."

Tino rubbed his neck, smiling in response, "Thank you for not doing that. I'd have been eaten for sure! But, you know, you've both told me plenty of times that the whole circus is like your own tiger. So, in a way, you did. I'd like to think I haven't given you any cause to regret it."

Leila laughed, too. "Well, I'm not sure Rita would agree…but I think everyone else is glad to have you around, Tino. You've been a great asset to the marketing team. Mom likes you well enough to keep letting you come to the home office for the season break, though she might change her mind if you don't take that software class this year and get up to speed."

Raj helped himself to coffee and pulled up a chair. "I know we're supposed to be concentrating on merchandise today, but before we start, I want to say how much I like the show's new YouTube channel, Tino. Who knew Francine would turn out to be such a star?"

"Do you think she'll take that job at the animal park?" Tino asked. "We we came up with some great stuff for the tiger brand together—I'll show it to you today—and I would really miss working with her."

Raj shrugged, and Tino could see the regret in his face. "You know, after having the spotlight for a while, I think she is ready to take the next step in her career." Raj's eyes were fixed on Leila.

"We'll keep her if we can, Raj," Leila said as she stood up and went over to her cabinet and pulled a file out. "I can offer her a little more money and a new job title. But we can't promote her without *promoting Dan, as well. It may just be her time to move on. We can't dwell on things we can't control, can we? Besides, we have our own challenges to cope with, right?"*

"True," replied Raj. "In fact, we should fill Tino in. Ruby called yesterday. There's a new Canadian show that's running the same basic tour route we are. Their budget for sets and costumes is huge, and they don't have any animals to feed. They could really get into our pockets this season."

"Yeah," Tino replied, "Leila was just telling me about that before you got here. Actually, I have some ideas that may help, thanks to the regional research I did at the home office. Did you know that there are two or three animal preserves close to our major stops that do small performances with elephants and some other exotics? Maybe we could invite them to join us for local shows, come up with some profit-sharing scenarios?...And there are several merchandise possibilities we haven't explored. Everyone loves the music we had composed for the show. Why don't we see about selling it via CD or MP3 on our website?"

"Now THAT'S an interesting idea," replied Leila. "Keep going."

An hour later, his marketing work done for the day, Tino hopped the trailer steps and started towards the tiger enclosure. He could hear one of them rumbling; it sounded like Bara's voice. He knew Raj planned to retire her at the end of the season, maybe earlier if the arthritis flared up again, but had not decided whether to replace her or make do with two cats. It seemed like several things they had all come to take for granted were now about to change. Would the life of the circus be threatened when those changes came? He wasn't sure.

But right now, the cats were restless and ready for some exercise, he bet. Dan would be waiting. Increasing his pace to an easy jog, Tino headed toward the enclosure. It was the world's best office, and he couldn't wait to get back to work.

🐾 🐾 🐾 🐾

Another year has gone by and the circus has completed another tour. Raj is back, Francine may be moving on, and Tino's moving up in the company. There is new competition on the horizon, and the organization may have to adjust to life without at least one of its star performers. While the ring master and tiger tamer have some of the best and most sustainable Plan-Act-Reflect-Refine-Act processes that Tino has ever seen, some of those challenges will likely be tough to meet. He knows that the organization has implemented best practices that offer the best chance of surviving in the face of inevitable change.

What is true for the Cirque Maravilla is going to be true everywhere. The show must go on. Every organization has a life cycle and will experience change over time. People come and go, economies change, and technology evolves. People change and move within the company and elsewhere. When a leadership position opens up, it has to be filled. The marketplace changes, and practices will have to change with them. Innovation occurs and the leadership will need to respond decisively and with good judgment.

But the essential nature of your organization — whether it is business, non-profit, or other — will not change. A tiger will be a tiger all its life. If you want to keep it roaring and jumping through those hoops, your commitment and effort must remain consistent. Your core values should not change. You should always affirm your dedication to key standards like quality, timeliness, great customer service, and honorable employee relations. Think of your operations as an ecosystem. You are responsible for maintaining the integrity of that ecosystem because your tiger's health depends on it.

Like Cirque Maravilla, your show also depends on your ability to properly cultivate the people or team that you have brought together. Just like we've watched Raj and Leila do, you too must grow the people in your business, including yourself. Keep everyone up to speed so they can perform at their peak. Decide which opportunities are the best fit for your own trajectory, and prepare yourself to lead. Keep identifying those with leadership potential. Remember, you will go away someday too - whether it's to take a sabbatical, another job opportunity, retirement, or the inevitable passing away of life. Make your time count.

What can Tino take away from his time with Raj and Leila that might help him face the facts of the circus's situation without losing faith in its ability to thrive?

- Have a strong vision. Make sure everyone in your organization knows your vision. Communicate your vision into achievable goals and show everyone in your organization how to contribute to execute this vision.

- Challenge that vision continually in a way that keeps it consistent, yet fresh and relevant.

- Give strategic planning the time, attention, and respect it deserves. Without it, tigers starve (or eat you up) and shows close down.

- Have a continuous improvement plan in place. There is nothing wrong with celebrating success. In fact, it's good for motivation and morale. But never allow your organization to get so satisfied or complacent that it loses the desire to grow or the willingness to improve.

Despite the discomfort that we are all inclined to feel in the face of uncertainty, we realize that Tino is a fortunate young man. He has a job that he loves, doing work that he finds satisfying and working with mentors he admires in an organization that he believes in passionately. Wouldn't you too in his situation believe that you're part of the Greatest Show on Earth?

ABOUT THE AUTHOR

Todd Shuler currently serves as Global Services Delivery Manager at TEKsystems Global Services LLC.

In the recent past, Mr. Shuler served as Director of Consulting Services at Apex Systems. He brings a stellar background of management consulting, business and IT Strategy and Implementation for both the private and public sectors having worked for such Big 3 Consulting powerhouses: Deloitte and Ernst & Young. He also previously worked for Citizant, Texas Instruments and Bank of America.

Todd has established a distinguished track record of service to many clients including the Air Force Reserve Command (AFRC), Bank of America, Bristol-Myers Squibb, Cargill, City of Macon, City of Philadelphia, Cultura Technologies, the U.S. Department of Homeland Security, Deutsche Bank, GEICO, Iezumi Printing Corporation (Tokyo, Japan), Landis & Gyr, Military Health Service (MHS) Options Clearing Corporation, State of Michigan, The Lowe's Companies and Thermo King (an Ingersoll-Rand company).

Mr. Shuler is also a veteran of the US Armed Forces where he served in Operation Desert Storm. Todd graduated from the Terry College of Business at the University of Georgia with a Bachelors of Business Administration in Management Information Systems with a minor in Japanese Language and Literature. He is currently pursuing his Masters of Divinity at Reformed Theological Seminary as well as his Masters of Business Administration (MBA) at the J. Whitney Bunting School of Business at Georgia College and State University.

---

[i] Steve Jobs' 2005 Stanford Commencement Address:
http://news.stanford.edu/news/2005/june15/jobs-061505.html

[ii] Robert Cooper, The Breaking of Nations: Order and Chaos in the Twenty-first Century (New York City, NY: Grove Press, 2004) p.77

[iii] Kudlow, L. (1999, March 8) "Interview with Jack Welch." Retrieved July 16, 2013 from http://www.realclearmarkets.com/articles/2009/03/an_interview_with_jack_welch.html

[iv] Hewitt, D. (Executive Producer). (2003) Interview with Steve Jobs. *60 Minutes* [Television broadcast]. New York: CBS News.

[v] Allen, Robert G. (2000, October). Enlightened Wealth Institute Info-marketing Teleconference